1,2,3 John

BOOKS IN THE BIBLE STUDY COMMENTARY SERIES

BIBLE STUDY COMMENTARY

1,2,3 John

CURTIS VAUGHAN

ZONDERVAN PUBLISHING HOUSE

OF THE ZONDERVAN CORPORATION
GRAND RAPIDS, MICHIGAN 49506

1, 2, 3, JOHN: A BIBLE STUDY COMMENTARY
© 1970 by The Zondervan Publishing House
Grand Rapids, Michigan

ISBN 0-310-33563-9

Library of Congress Catalog Card Number: 74-120037

Printed in the United States of America

83 84 85 86 87 88 — 20 19 18 17 16 15 14 13

Contents

2/032

Introduction

The five books of the New Testament which have been traditionally ascribed to John the apostle (the fourth gospel, three epistles, and Revelation) may "represent the highest reach of inspiration and revelation in our New Testament" (D. A. Hayes, p. 72). Yet the New Testament tells us surprisingly little about their author. He is mentioned by name only three times in Matthew, ten times in Mark, seven times in Luke, nine times in Acts, one time in Galatians, and five times in Revelation. In most of these references there is the mere mention of the name, and little or no information is given about the man.

We do not know when or where he was born, but we do know some things about his family. For instance, we know that he had a brother named James, that his father's name was Zebedee, and that his mother's name was Salome. (Some believe that the mother of John was a sister of Mary the mother of Jesus [cf. John 19:25; Mark 15:40]). In addition, we know that the family was engaged in the fishing industry. That the family was well-to-do is suggested by the fact that they had hired servants (Mark 1:20), that the mother in the family was one of the women who ministered to Jesus of their substance (Mark 15:41; Luke 8:3), and that John appears to have been known to the high priest and had access to the high priest's court at the time of the arrest of Jesus (John 18:15-16). In addition, there is at least the suggestion that John had a home in Jerusalem (Matt. 20:20), which would be most unusual for a simple Galilean fisherman who for several years had not been actively engaged in his business. It is logical to conclude that he had some independent resources upon which to draw.

Tradition has it that John remained in Jerusalem until the death of Mary, the mother of Jesus, which is said to have occurred near the middle of the first century. Irenaeus informs us that John later took up residence in Ephesus. The early church believed that the fourth gospel and the three epistles were all written while he was living in that city.

Tradition is unanimous in its testimony that John outlived all the other apostles, dying in the city of Ephesus at an advanced age.

7

Jerome, for instance, says that the apostle lived sixty-eight years after the crucifixion. That would put his death somewhere around A.D. 100.

1 JOHN

Characteristics of the Letter

To understand I John one needs to be aware of certain pertinent facts about it. Some of these are as follows:

1. *It is a general letter.* Most of Paul's letters were written to particular churches or individuals. But such was not the case with I John. It doubtless was intended for the churches of the province of Asia, but apart from allusions to a particular heresy, there is a complete lack of local color. No personal details are given; not a single name (other than the name of our Lord) occurs in it; it has no salutation and no final greetings. Indeed, it reads more like a treatise than a letter. The only real clue to the destination of the letter is in the relationship implied between the author and his readers.

2. *It is a difficult letter.* Perhaps it is, as Alford says, the most difficult of all the New Testament epistles. The style, the structure, the thought — all of these contribute to its complexity. Admittedly, even the most unsophisticated reader can derive immeasurable benefit merely by a casual reading of the epistle. But even the greatest theologians and the most skilled exegetes are unable to grasp the message of John in its deepest meaning.

3. *It is a crisis letter,* having been written to stem the tide of a deadly doctrinal error which threatened to destroy the fellowship of the churches of Asia. This controversy is reflected in nearly every verse of the letter, but its distinctive features are most clearly delineated in 2:18-28 and 4:1-6. It is universally agreed that the error in question was some form of gnosticism, a quasi-philosophical movement which had its beginnings in the latter part of the first Christian century and came to full flower in the middle of the second century.

Gnosticism was essentially a combination of oriental mysticism and Greek philosophy. Eventually, it took on just enough of Christianity to make it a formidable foe to the faith. John considered it a counterfeit Christianity and viewed its growth "with unconcealed anxiety and open abhorrence" (Ramsay, p. 35).

The following are the principal tenets of gnosticism: (1) It made knowledge, not faith, the one condition of salvation and the only test of fellowship with God. This knowledge, however, was not open to everyone but was the privilege only of those who had been initiated into the mysteries of the gnostic system. It was therefore an esoteric knowledge to which simple believers could not attain. This distorted emphasis on knowledge led to arrogance, lovelessness, and exclusivism. It also gave to the movement its name, the Greek word for knowledge being *gnosis*.

(2) It taught that all matter is inherently evil. This doctrine, in turn, led the gnostics into at least two other very grave errors, one practical and the other theological. The *practical* error concerned the nature of the Christian life. Starting with the assumption that the body is evil, some gnostics turned to asceticism and others to the opposite extreme of licentiousness. It appears that licentiousness was the tendency of those whom John opposes in this epistle. The body, they argued, is evil and doomed to sin, but the spirit is independent of the body, and therefore remains undefiled regardless of what one does. By this reasoning they set themselves above the obligations of morality and insisted that for them nothing was sin.

Theologically, the gnostic belief in the inherent evil of matter led to an outright denial of the real Incarnation of God in Christ. Their contention was that the divine Word could not be united with a human body, for the body, to them, was evil. They explained away the Incarnation in one of two ways. Some did so by denying the actual humanity of Jesus, holding that He only *seemed* to be human. The body of Jesus was an illusion, a phantom, only apparently real. Others explained away the Incarnation by denying the real deity of Jesus. This form of the heresy (sometimes called Cerinthianism because it was taught by Cerinthus, a contemporary of John) made a distinction between the man Jesus and the divine Christ. They held that Jesus was a mere man born through the usual generative process. Joseph was His father; Mary was His mother. He was distinguished above other men in character, but was still only a man. The heavenly Christ (called by the gnostics an *aeon*) came upon the man Jesus at His baptism but left Him before His death on the cross. The Christ, therefore, was not actually born and did not really suffer. It was the man Jesus who was born, and it was the man Jesus who died. He was not, in their thinking, the Son of God. The Son of God was the heavenly Christ who, for only a season, had been united with the man Jesus.

Every sentence of I John reflects the apostle's abhorrence of the gnostic system. He taught that it was wholly subversive of

Christianity and that no compromise whatsoever could be made with it.

4. *It is a companion letter to the gospel.* Biblical scholars differ in their understanding of the relationship of the epistle to the gospel, but all are agreed that the two works are linked together by style, vocabulary, characteristic phrases, and fundamental concepts. Brooke quotes Schulze to the effect that "in the whole of the first Epistle there is hardly a single thought that is not found in the Gospel" (p. ix).

It is open to debate whether the gospel or the epistle comes first, or whether they were written at one and the same time. Those who believe the epistle was written before the gospel support their position with the assertion that the epistle is shorter, simpler, and more primitive in its theological emphases. The epistle, in their thinking, is a sort of preliminary sketch of the theology of the gospel of John.

Most scholars hold that the epistle was written after the gospel. Brooke, for instance, sees the epistle as "a summary, not a first sketch" of the gospel (p. xxvi). "Many passages of the Epistle," he says, "seem to need the help of the Gospel in order to become intelligible" (pp. xxii-xxiii).

Still a third group of scholars holds (correctly, we believe) that the epistle was written about the same time as the gospel and sent along with the gospel as a companion writing. Blaiklock, a proponent of this view, says the epistle "was written to accompany and introduce the Gospel. That is why the two books should always be read side by side in mutual commentary. The letter dealt more directly with the spiritual problems of the hour, and attacked error in a manner which would have been out of place in the Gospel. The letter formed a sermon upon the Gospel" (p. 9).

5. *It is a late letter.* Indeed, it may well have been the last writing of the New Testament. But whether or not this is so, many things in the book point to a period toward the close of the first Christian century: the nature of the heresy combatted, the indications that the author was an aged man to whom all his readers were "little children," the suggestion that a second or third generation of believers had come to be, and so on.

Ramsay concludes that "the direct evidences supplied by the Epistle are very slight, and all that can be said with certainty is that the writing must be placed at a late date, but so far as the witness of the Epistle goes, it may well fall within the first century, not far from its close" (p. 41).

Plan of the Letter

Some of the ancient interpreters saw no order at all in I John and thought of the writer simply as a contemplative mystic who wrote down his meditations in the form of detached and isolated sayings. In the modern period scholars have correctly discerned connected order in the epistle, but there has been a tendency to be too exact and minute in tracing out the thought of the writer.

All outlines of I John are to a large extent artificial, but perhaps, as Plummer remarks, it is better to read the book "under the guidance of any scheme that will at all coincide with its contents, than with no guidance whatever" (p. liv). The main body of the epistle, which begins at 1:5, may be seen as containing three movements or cycles. The first, which represents the Christian life as *a divine fellowship,* shows that righteousness, love, and adherence to the truth are marks of those who are in the fellowship (1:5—2:28). The second movement introduces the thought of the Christian life as *a divine sonship,* and righteousness, love, and adherence to the truth are presented as evidences of this filial relationship to God (2:29—4:6). The third movement (4:7—5:20) is difficult to analyze, but it appears to be *a general discussion* of some of the leading ideas of the epistle. In it John mentions love, faith, righteousness, sonship, assurance, and so on. He looks at these things from various angles and shows how they are related to one another.

In the exposition to follow we have sought to isolate the larger units of thought and to develop and explain them without reference to an overall scheme. For a full analysis of the thought of the epistle the reader is referred to the works of Robert Law, B. F. Westcott, and Alfred Plummer. Law is particularly incisive and has had tremendous influence upon those who have written on I John since his book made its appearance.

What George G. Findlay says of John's treatment of divine love in a large sense holds true of the overall style of this epistle. That is to say, the apostle takes a theme and "holds it up as a jewel to the sun; each turn of expression, like another facet, flashes out some new ray of heavenly light" (p. 327).

THE TWO SHORTER EPISTLES

These two letters, which D. A. Hayes calls "specimens of the less important religious correspondence of the apostolic age" (p. 205), belonged to the *antilegomena* (disputed books) of the New Testament. That is to say, in the early period of Christian history there was not complete agreement as to their canonicity. They were not included in the ancient Syriac New Testament and were rarely referred to by the early church fathers. These facts, however, do not necessarily reflect doubt concerning the apostolic origin of the letters. They are of such slight size and so personal in character that they were probably not widely known.

These two epistles are the shortest books in the New Testament. Each of them contains less than 250 words in Greek and could easily be written on a single sheet of papyrus (cf. II John 12). Findlay describes them as "notes snatched from the every-day correspondence of an apostle" (p. 4). Neither of them contains very much that cannot be found in I John. Indeed, II John has been described as a "cut-down" version of the first epistle.

Both letters are pastoral in tone and may in this regard be compared with the letters to Timothy, Titus, and Philemon. They deal with orthodoxy, church order, and Christian hospitality. Second John warns against extending hospitality to the enemies of the Gospel; III John commends Gaius for the practice of hospitality in reference to true "brethren."

Their chief value for us is that they furnish insights into the historical setting of the first epistle.

Notes on 2 John

INTRODUCTION (verses 1-3)

Verse 1. *Elder* may be used either as an official title (cf. I Pet. 5:1) or in the sense of "old man." Many modern interpreters understand *the elect lady* to be a reference to a church. More convincing arguments may be made for the view that the reference is to a Christian ("elect") woman. The TCNT: "an eminent Christian lady." Goodspeed: "the chosen lady." Some think the word translated "lady" should be read as a proper name ("Kyria" or "Cyria"). *Whom,* which is masculine in Greek, includes both the elect lady and her children. *Truth,* which here means "sincerity" is one of the key words of this epistle (cf. verses 1, 2, 3, 4). *The truth* (last occurrence, verse 1) is the truth of the Gospel, the revelation of God in Christ.

Verse 3. *Be* is better translated "shall be" (ASV). The verse is not a prayer or a wish but a statement of confident assurance. *Love* is another key word of this epistle, being found twice as a noun and twice as a verb.

I. Occasion of the Letter (verse 4)

John had come across some of the elect lady's children in the course of his travels and had been favorably impressed by their conduct. *Of thy children,* that is, "some of your children" (TCNT).

II. Exhortations and Warnings (verses 5-11)

1. *Exhortation to love and obedience* (5-6)

Verse 5. Compare I John 3:7.

Verse 6. "To live by his commandments, that is what love means" (Moffatt).

Verse 7. *Deceivers* are those who lead others astray, cause them to wander from the truth. The TCNT says, "impostors." The reference is to the gnostic teachers. On antichrist see I John 2:18 ff.

2. *Warnings against false doctrine* (verses 7-9)

Verse 8. The *things which we have wrought* refers to the labors of John and others in building these people up in the faith. Phillips: "don't throw away all the labor that has been spent on you."

The full reward is the reward of the faithful to be meted out in the last day. The TCNT, with less likelihood, interprets it in the sense of the full benefit of the labor spent on the readers: "reap the benefit of it in full."

Verse 9. *Whosoever transgresseth.* Better, "Whosoever goeth onward" (ASV). The words may mean "everyone who sets himself up as a leader" (cf. Berkeley). More probably, however, the reference is to "everyone who goes beyond the truth (the gospel)" (cf. TCNT). The errorists doubtless thought of themselves as "progressives," as "advanced" thinkers. On *he hath both the Father and the Son* see I John 2:22-23.

3. *Warning against helping heretical teachers* (verses 10-11)

Verse 10. *If there come any unto you,* that is, on a mission as a teacher. The reference is to the false teachers.

Conclusion (verses 12-13)

Verse 12. *Paper*: a sheet of papyrus. Perhaps John means that his letter must come to an end because he has used up his papyrus. *That our* ["your," ASV] *joy may be made full*: compare I John 1:4.

Verse 13. *Elect sister*: a Christian lady, sister to the lady mentioned in verse 1.

Notes on 3 John

I. SALUTATION (verse 1)

The elder. See on II John 1. *Gaius* was perhaps the most common of all names in the Roman Empire (Plummer). In the New Testament there was a Gaius of Macedonia (Acts 19:29), of Derbe (Acts 20:4), and of Corinth (Rom. 16:23). This is perhaps still another person bearing that name.

II. PRAYER AND COMMENDATION FOR GAIUS (verses 2-8)

Verse 2. *Above all things*: "in all things" (ASV) relating to Gaius' physical and temporal well being.

Soul: the immaterial part of being.

Verse 3. *The truth that is in thee.* Better, "thy truth" (ASV) or "the sincerity of your life" (Phillips). *Came* and *testified* mean "repeatedly came" and "repeatedly bore witness."

Verse 4. *In truth.* Better, "the truth" (RSV). Note recurrence of "truth" in the first three verses.

Verse 5. *Thou doest faithfully.* Literally, "a faithful work" (ASV). *To the brethren, and to strangers.* The NEB says, "for these our fellow Christians, strangers though they are to you." The thought is that Gaius showed hospitality toward the brethren even when those brethren were strangers.

Verse 6. *Before the church,* that is, the church at Ephesus (or wherever John was at the time of writing this letter). *After a godly sort*: The meaning is "in a manner worthy of the service of God" (TCNT) or in a manner which is in keeping with the fact that the work is God's work.

Verse 7. The *name* is the name of Jesus (cf. Acts 5:41).

Taking nothing denotes customary action. *Gentiles*: pagans, those who do not know God.

Verse 8: *We* is emphatic, "we Christians."

III. WARNING ABOUT DIOTREPHES (verses 9-11)

Verse 9 may contain a reference to II John. Many, however, think that the reference is to a lost letter. *Diotrephes* is mentioned nowhere else in the New Testament. He may have been the pastor of the church. *Who loveth to have the pre-eminence*: "who loves to have the foremost place" (Weymouth). *Receiveth us not* means "does not acknowledge our (John's) authority." Rotherham translates it, "doth not make us welcome."

Verse 10. A threat to call public attention to Diotrephes. *Prating*: literally, "boiling over." Plummer takes it to mean something like "talking nonsense." *Receive the brethren*: show hospitality to them.

Verse 11. Diotrephes' conduct is an example of that which must not be imitated.

IV. COMMENDATION OF DEMETRIUS (verse 12)

Demetrius, whom John commends to the hospitality of Gaius, may have been the bearer of this letter. His credentials are of the highest sort: he has "the witness of all men, and of the truth itself" (ASV), and of John. The only other occurrence of the name in the New Testament is of the silversmith who opposed Paul in Ephesus (Acts 19:24).

Two explanations are given of *the truth*: (1) revealed truth as the rule of life, (2) the Spirit of truth which is within the believer (Plummer).

CONCLUSION (verses 13-14)

Verse 13. *Pen*: a reed for writing.

FOR FURTHER STUDY

1. Read I John in a modern translation. Mark passages indicating John's purpose in writing his epistle.

2. Read articles on John in a Bible dictionary. *The Zondervan Pictorial Bible Dictionary* and *The New Bible Dictionary* (Eerdmans) are good one-volume works.

3. Using a concordance, look up every New Testament passage in which John is mentioned by name.

4. Read the article on I John in *The New International Bible Encyclopedia*. This is an especially helpful article.

5. Read the article on Gnosticism in *The New Bible Dictionary*.

6. For sermonic material on the epistles of John see Vol. 4 of Spurgeon's *Treasury of the New Testament* (Zondervan) and Maclaren's *Expositions of Holy Scripture* (Eerdmans). Spurgeon has nearly 150 large double-column pages of sermons on I John.

CHAPTER ONE

The Word of Life

(1 John 1:1-4)

I. The Apostolic Proclamation (1:1-3)
   1. The substance of the proclamation (1-3a)
      (1) His pre-existent glory
      (2) His real humanity
      (3) His manifested life
   2. The purpose of the proclamation (3)
II. The Purpose of the Epistle (4)

First John has no epistolary introduction such as we find in most New Testament letters. This suggests that it is not as much a letter as an informal homily. Its tone is that of a pastor addressing his congregation.

The book opens with a prologue which, in some respects, is reminiscent of the first eighteen verses of the gospel of John. There are striking parallels in phrasing (e.g., "That which was from the beginning," "In the beginning was the Word") and in the use of characteristic words (e.g. "Word," "life," "witness"). Moreover, the two passages are concerned with the same central figure, namely, Jesus as the Word of God.

There is, however, a difference in emphasis. The prologue to the gospel emphasizes the eternal nature of the Word, His deity, and His agency in creation, as background for the assertion that "the Word became flesh and dwelt among us" (John 1:14). The epistle, on the other hand, acknowledges the deity of the Word but puts stress on His real humanity.

The prologue to the epistle is not as long nor as profound nor as majestic as the prologue to the gospel, but it is nonetheless a statement of great weight and power. Some see it as the pivotal statement on which the whole epistle is built.

This introductory paragraph may be divided into two parts. Verses 1-3 are a general description of the apostolic proclamation; verse 4 sets forth the purpose of this epistle.

I. THE APOSTOLIC PROCLAMATION (1:1-3)

In the Greek text, as well as in most of the English translations, the first three verses constitute one long, complicated sentence.[1] Sawtelle says, "The apostle has so much to crowd into his opening sentence that he seems scarcely to know how to begin" (p. 5). Every word is freighted with meaning.

If we are to follow the train of thought, it is essential that we understand the *structure* of the sentence. Three things are to be observed: First, the *main verb* ("declare") is found in verse 3. The object of this verb is expressed by four relative clauses which, for the sake of emphasis, are placed at the beginning of the sentence in verse 1. The essential statement therefore is as follows: "We declare to you that which was from the beginning, that which we have heard, that which we have seen with our eyes, that which we beheld and our hands handled concerning the Word of life."[2]

The declaration summarized in these verses is taken by many to be a sort of recapitulation of the gospel of John. This idea is particularly attractive if we assume, as many do, that I John was written as a covering letter for the gospel and dispatched simultaneously with it. Others prefer to think of the declaration mentioned here as more general; that is, as a summary of the total apostolic proclamation, oral and written.

Second, all of verse 2 is a *parenthesis*. It explains how the declaration set out in verse 1 is possible. Two matters are emphasized: (1) "the life" with which that declaration is concerned has been historically manifested. (2) John's own personal experience confirmed it: "We have seen it, and bear witness."

Third, the words placed at the beginning of verse 3 ("that which we have seen and heard") are *resumptive*. That is to say, they pick

---

[1]George G. Findlay's analysis of these verses is different and quite suggestive. He takes the opening phrase ("that which was from the beginning") to be complete in itself and accordingly places a period at the end of the phrase. Another period is put at the end of verse 1 and the whole of the verse is read as a sort of title to the epistle. Moreover, by construing verse 1 in this fashion, Findlay is able to remove the parentheses from verse 2. He sees that verse not "as an eddy in the current" but rather as "the centre of the passage" (pp. 83-84).

[2]The phrase "concerning the word of life" (ASV) may be construed in any one of several ways: as a sort of resume of the four preceding clauses and standing in apposition with them — "all that concerns the word of life"; as a modifier of "have heard" (and loosely all the verbs following "have heard"); or as a modifier of "declare" (verse 3).

up anew and repeat in part the statement begun in verse 1. After the long parenthesis of verse 2, John felt that clarity of thought made it appropriate for him thus to repeat himself.

Having considered the structure of verses 1-3, it is now necessary to consider in greater detail what is taught in these verses about the apostolic proclamation. Two matters are presented: (1) the substance of the proclamation (verses 1-3a) and (2) the purpose of it (verse 3b).

1. *The substance of the proclamation* (verses 1-3a). The heart of the apostolic announcement is found in the expression *the Word of life* (verse 1). There are two lines of interpretation. First, there are those (e.g. Westcott, Findlay, Brooke, Dodd, Barclay) who interpret the expression as being impersonal. These take "Word" to mean something like "account" or "preaching" or "announcement" or as Westcott puts it, the "whole message from God to man." "Life" is construed as an objective genitive. Thus, in this interpretation, the "Word of life" is the revelation or announcement of life. "It is," in Findlay's words, "synonymous with 'the Gospel,' the message of the new life which those bear witness to and report who have first 'heard' it and proved its life-giving power" (p. 83). (Compare John 6:68; Phil. 2:16.)

The use of the neuter relative pronoun (translated "that which" in verse 1) gives some support to this view. Another matter which seems to lend strength to this interpretation is the fact that the stress of the phrase is on "life" rather than on "Word." Immediately after mentioning the "Word of life" John continues by saying, "For the *life* was manifested" (verse 2).

The other interpretation sees "the Word of life" as personal, that is, as a reference to the Son of God who is the revelation or expression of God to man. (Note the use of a capital letter in KJV and ASV, "the Word.") This is the interpretation of Calvin, Alford, Plummer, Law, Conner, Ross, and many others. Those who hold this view refer to John's use of "Word" as a name for Christ in the opening verses of his gospel and the similar use of the term in Revelation 19:13. On the whole it seems the better way of looking at the matter.

In this interpretation "life" may be taken as a descriptive (attributive) genitive ("the living Word," "the life-giving Word") or as an appositional genitive ("the Word who is the life").

What is proclaimed about the Word of life may be summarized as follows:

(1) *His pre-existent glory.* Some interpreters who explain

"Word of life" as a reference to the gospel take *that which was from the beginning* (verse 1a) as a statement designed simply to remove all thought of novelty in the apostolic announcement. It was, they aver, the writer's way of saying that what he has to announce about the Word of life is no new discovery.

"The beginning" in this approach may be understood as a reference to creation, the beginning of history, or to the Incarnation, the beginning of the gospel age. There is, however, more to John's words than this interpretation permits. "From the beginning" is to be understood as practically equivalent to "from eternity." The wording, to be sure, is not identical with John 1:1, but the idea seems to be essentially the same in the two passages. In light of this, "that which was from the beginning" should be seen as a reference to something about the Word (Christ) which antedates time. Calvin takes it to be "the divinity of Christ" (p. 158). Alford explains the whole statement to mean Christ's "eternal pre-existence and inherent Life and Glory with the Father" (p. 1694).

The neuter ("that which") rather than the masculine ("him who") is used because the declaration was not simply of the person of Christ but of all that relates to Him. Paul writes similarly in I Corinthians 15:10: "By the grace of God I am *what* I am."

"Was" translates a Greek imperfect tense and suggests what always has been. Christ the Word did not come to be at some point in time; He already was when time began. He "was" before He "was manifested" (cf. John 1:1, 14).

(2) *His real humanity*: "That which we have heard . . . seen . . . beheld . . . handled, concerning the Word of life . . . declare we unto you" (verses 1b-3a, ASV). This statement serves a dual purpose. For one thing, by an impressive accumulation of words, it affirms and emphasizes the real humanity of Christ. This emphasis on His physical tangibility was doubtless directed against the reckless and unfounded claims of the Gnostics. These heretical teachers combined pagan philosophy and superstition with just enough Christianity to make their system especially dangerous. They denied a real Incarnation, some of them teaching that Jesus was merely a phantom, that He seemed to be a man but was not really a man. John, on the other hand, teaches that in Jesus the eternal God actually clothed Himself in human flesh and made Himself real to men through their senses. John and others heard Him speak, saw Him with their eyes, touched Him with their hands. In John's thinking God came all the way down to us. He took our nature; He became a man of flesh and blood.

Moreover, these words show that the first preachers of the Gospel were reliable and authoritative witnesses of the truth which they proclaimed. Indeed, this emphasis pervades the entire sentence which makes up the first three verses. Three times the writer asserts "we have seen"; twice he writes "we have heard"; and twice he declares that the life "was manifested." John's readers, who belonged to a later generation and had never seen Jesus, might have had questions about the apostolic message. The apostle takes great pains to assure them that he and his fellow apostles were competent witnesses and that what they proclaimed was trustworthy and true. He seems to struggle for words strong enough to express his feelings. "I tell you," he says, "we saw these things with our own eyes, we heard them with our own ears, we have touched and tested them at every point, and we know beyond any doubt that they are so."

Before leaving the first verse attention should be called to the significance of its verbs. "Was," as noted above, translates a Greek imperfect tense and may suggest what always has been. The verbs translated "we have heard" and "we have seen" are both perfect tenses. They point up the abiding reality of the audible and visible experiences of the apostle which may have occurred frequently. What was seen and heard during the days of Christ's earthly ministry left an abiding impression on him. "With our eyes" are words added to the verb "have seen" to emphasize that the experience was actual.

The verbs translated "we beheld" and "our hands handled" introduce a sudden change in tense. In the Greek both are in the aorist tense, possibly referring to a single act (in contrast with the oft-repeated acts of the two preceding verbs). Some interpreters think they refer to some special occasion when John and his fellow apostles had the experience described here. Specifically, the allusion may be to a time when they looked upon and handled the glorified body of the risen Christ (cf. Luke 24:39; John 20:27). Others doubt that the statement can legitimately be confined to a post-resurrection experience.

"We beheld" translates a word which speaks of an intent, contemplative gaze. Barclay says it means "to gaze at someone, or something, until a long look has grasped something of the meaning and significance of that person or thing" (p. 27). In earlier Greek usage it suggested looking with a sense of wonder, but by New Testament times the word had lost this significance. John uses it in the prologue to his gospel when he writes of Jesus, "We beheld his glory" (John 1:14). Jesus used it when addressing the multitudes about John the Baptist: "What went ye out into the wilderness to behold?"

(Luke 7:24, ASV). In the epistle John uses it in two other places, 4:12 and 14.

"Handled," according to Findlay, "denoted not the bare *handling,* but the exploring use of the hands that *tests by handling*" (p. 85). It is found elsewhere in the New Testament only in Luke 24:39 ("handle"); Acts 17:27 ("feel after"); and Hebrews 12:18 ("touched"). In Genesis 27:12 the Septuagint uses it of the fumbling of a blind man. In Deuteronomy 28:29; Job 5:14; and 12:25 it is used of groping in the dark. Ross comments: "Now that the Eternal Logos has been manifested, we no longer fumble in the dark, feeling after God; in Christ we have grasped hold of reality" (p. 135).

(3) *His manifested life.* Verse 2, a parenthesis, explains how it was possible for men to see, hear, and handle the eternal Word. It was because the Word (Christ) in His character as the life, became visible: *For the life was manifested, and we have seen it, and bear witness, and shew unto you that eternal life, which was with the Father, and was manifested unto us* (verse 2). These words are spoken of "the life," but the context suggests that the "life" and the "Word" are one. This is borne out by the similar statement in John 1:4: "In him [i.e., the Word] was life; and the life was the light of men." (See also I John 5:20 [". . . and we are in him that is true, even in his Son Jesus Christ. This is the true God, and eternal life"]; and John 14:6 ["I am . . . the life"]). "Life," then, like "Word" in verse 1, is a name for Christ.[3]

The key word is "manifested," used twice in this verse. A term of frequent occurrence in the New Testament, it is employed most often of God or Christ, or of men in relation to God and Christ. Westcott calls attention to its use in John's writings of Christ's first coming (I John 3:5, 8; John 1:31), of His revelation after the Resurrection (John 21:1, 14), and of His Second Coming (I John 2:28). Essentially it means "to bring to light," "to make known that which already exists." Thus the life which always existed in the divine Word was in Jesus made tangible and visible. The verse begins with an unqualified declaration of this fact. The last part of the verse repeats the idea with one addition: the Life was manifested "unto us."

The thought expressed by "manifested" corresponds with "the

---

[3]Calvin, who explains "Word of life" to mean "life-giving Word," prefers to interpret "life" here not as a personal name for Christ but as a reference to the life which is offered us in Christ.

Word was made flesh" (John 1:14). There is, however, this difference: "the Word was made flesh" focuses on the Incarnation as *a historic event.* "The life was manifested" suggests the *unfolding* of Christ's incarnate life. What we are saying is that the manifestation of the life was the consequence, the outworking, of the Incarnation. Lenski understands the phrase to include "the whole manifestation from the incarnation to the ascension" but thinks it has special reference to the period "from the baptism until the ascension, the time when the apostles beheld his glory" (p. 37).

Three things are said of the life manifested in Christ: (1) The life is "eternal life" (verse 2b; literally, "the life, the eternal," which is a stronger way of putting the idea). The adjective attributes to the life a quality that transcends time, that cannot be measured by time. (2) The life was "with the Father" (verse 2c). The Greek construction implies a personal, face-to-face relationship. (3) John was witness to the life (verse 2a). "Have seen" (which sums up the four verbs of verse 1), "bear witness," and "show" (better, "declare") all relate in some way to this thought. The three terms speak, respectively, of experience, testimony, and announcement.

2. *The purpose of the proclamation* (verse 3). The apostolic witness was given with compassionate concern for those who heard it. "That which we have seen and heard declare we unto you, *that ye also may have fellowship with us*" (verse 3a). Those who are really in the divine fellowship cannot be satisfied while there are others still on the outside. As Spurgeon comments, "Having found the honey, we cannot eat it alone; having tasted that the Lord is gracious, it is one of the first instincts of the newborn nature to send us out crying, 'Ho, every one that thirsteth, come ye to the waters, and he that hath no money: come ye, buy and eat; yea, come, buy wine and milk without money and without price' " (p. 478).

As explained above, these words resume the thought begun in verse 1 and which was interrupted by the parenthesis of the second verse. John repeats just enough of verse 1 ("that which we have seen and heard") to make the connection clear.

"Have fellowship" might have been expressed in Greek by a single word, but John uses here a verb and a noun. The expression therefore is an especially strong one, conveying the notion of the *enjoyment* of fellowship rather than the mere *fact* of fellowship. The verb, a present subjunctive literally meaning "continue to have," may contain a tacit allusion to the erroneous teaching which was threatening to destroy the fellowship of the Asian Christians. If we assume that the verb has this significance, John, in effect, says: "We are making our announcement to you in order that the fellowship may be kept intact, that is, that you may *go on having* fellowship with us." The context, however, gives more probability to the view that the verb means "have and continue to have." That is to say, the proclamation is made in order that men might enter the Christian fellowship and then continuously enjoy it.

"Fellowship" is one of the great words of the New Testament, even though it does not appear with unusual frequency. Altogether it is used twenty times, four of these occurrences being in I John. It calls to mind a tremendously important truth, namely, that the Christian life is not a life lived in isolation. It is a life common to and shared by all believers. This is an emphasis sorely needed in our day, for the "church" idea is under attack as perhaps it never has been. And many professing believers who do not vocally attack the church are quite indifferent to any real fellowship in it. Barrett wrote some years ago (and his words are doubly true today): "The greatest revival needed today is a revival of the sense of the importance and value of Church life to the individual believer" (p. 31). We would do well to remind ourselves that it was the concept of true Christian fellowship, a thing utterly foreign to ancient pagan society, that helped Christianity spread like a prairie fire throughout the Roman world.

The root meaning of the word is participation, that is, a sharing in something with others. Mrs. Montgomery has the word "partnership." The NEB translates the whole phrase, "so that we together may share in a common life."

John defines the fellowship as a fellowship among Christians ("with us"), but he insists that it is far more than this. "Truly our fellowship is *with the Father, and with his Son Jesus Christ*" (verse 3b). There is a solemn fullness about this statement. Plummer renders the Greek thus: "Our fellowship is with the Father, and with the Son of Him, Jesus Christ." He then points out that "both the preposition and the definite article are repeated, marking emphatically the distinction and equality between the Son and the Father." The title given our Lord is also worthy of notice. "Son" points up His sharing in the essence and glory of deity and emphasizes His capacity to reveal God. "Jesus" calls attention to the reality of His human life; "Christ" refers to His divine commission.

II. THE PURPOSE OF THE EPISTLE (verse 4)

John states the purpose of his epistle in verse 4: "And these things write we unto you *that your joy may be made full.*" The RSV says: "And we are writing this that our joy may be complete." This statement of purpose should be compared with 5:13, where John expresses the purpose of his letter in other terms. The two passages are complementary not contradictory. The words of the present passage are an echo of the words of Christ in John 15:11, "These things have I spoken unto you, that my joy might remain in you, and that your joy might be full."

Most commentaries take the "we" as a literary or editorial plural. Lenski, however, following Zahn, rejects this. He argues that John here, as in the first person plurals of verses 1-3, is speaking in the name of all the apostles. "These things," then, "includes the entire New Testament literature" (p. 380).

It is almost impossible to decide whether the true text read "your joy" (KJV) or "our joy" (RSV). Both yield a good sense. KJV refers to the joy of John's readers. The RSV suggests that John felt his own joy would be incomplete unless shared by his readers. The words of Samuel Rutherford reflect the same idea:

> Oh! if one soul from Anwoth
>   Meet me at God's right hand,
> My heaven will be two heavens
>   In Immanuel's land.

"Made full," translating a Greek perfect tense, suggests the idea of a joy made permanently full. "It is but the beginning of joy when we begin to believe. When faith daily increases, joy increases in proportion" (Luther).

The sequence of thought between fellowship (verse 3) and fullness of joy (verse 4) is significant. The import of it is that fullness of joy depends on the realization of true fellowship in Christ. "The isolated and solitary Christian can never be a happy Christian" (Barrett, p. 35).

For Further Study

1. Read I John in a translation you have not used before. Watch for recurring words such as "love," "know," etc.

2. Read articles on "Word" and "Fellowship" in *The Zondervan Pictorial Bible Dictionary*.

3. Using a concordance, check John's use of the word "manifest."

CHAPTER TWO

The Divine Fellowship

(1 John 1:5—2:6)

Throughout this section the Christian life is represented as a fellowship — both with other believers and with God.[1] The idea was introduced in 1:3, where the express purpose of the apostolic witness is said to be to bring men into a redemptive fellowship. This fellowship, the sharing in a common spiritual life, is in the truest sense a fellowship "with the Father, and with his Son Jesus Christ" (1:3b).

The English term, as stated in the preceding study, translates a Greek word (*koinonia*) which is used four times in I John (twice in 1:3, once in 1:6, and once in 1:7). Elsewhere in the New Testament the word occurs sixteen times (chiefly in the epistles of Paul). In the KJV it is translated by several different words, but "fellowship" and "communion" are the two principal ones. The word

---

[1]Several other expressions are used in the paragraph to describe the believer's relation to God, such as "knowing" God (2:3), "being in" him (2:5), and "abiding in" him (2:6). Fellowship, however, seems to be the dominant motif.

27

sometimes emphasized the idea of association or close relationship. Accordingly, some secular writers on occasion used it of the marital relationship. (A related word [*koinonos*] was a technical term for a business partner.) However, the root meaning of John's word is not association, but participation, a sharing in something with others. For example, Philemon 6 speaks of participation in the faith; Philippians 3:10, of participation in Christ's sufferings; II Corinthians 8:4, of sharing in the relief of the saints; II Corinthians 13:14, of participation in the Holy Spirit; I Corinthians 10:16, of participation in the blood of Christ; and so forth.

John's teaching concerning the Christian's fellowship with God may be summed up under four leading ideas: (1) fellowship and the character of God (1:5-7); (2) fellowship and confession (1:8-10); (3) fellowship and Christ's advocacy (2:1-2); (4) fellowship and obedience (2:3-6).

I. FELLOWSHIP AND THE CHARACTER OF GOD (1:5-7)

The character of God necessarily determines the character of fellowship with Him. Indeed, as Ramsay writes, "If we lose sight of the ethical nature of God, we miss the truth on which all Christianity is based and land in moral confusion. The purity of the Christian corresponds to the purity of God. Without this moral kinship there is no fellowship" (p. 249). John therefore prefaces this entire section with a profound declaration concerning the nature of God: *This then is the message which we have heard of him, and declare unto you, that God is light, and in him is no darkness at all* (1:5).

The first part of the verse might better be rendered, "And the message which we have heard from him and announce to you is this." The statement is possibly designed to call attention to the importance of what John is about to write. Conner likens it to Jesus' "verily, verily" (a formula, by the way, found only in John's gospel).

Verse 5 speaks of the origin of the message, the reporting of the message, and the substance of the message. Verses 6 and 7 affirm a logical conclusion drawn from the message.

1. *The origin of the message* (verse 5). John claims that his announcement concerning God is a "message which we have heard of him." The "him" refers to Christ who has been the main subject of the preceding verses. The Greek preposition rendered "of" could mark either the ultimate, or the immediate, source of the message. John was probably thinking of Christ as the immediate rather than the ultimate source. Ultimately the truth concerning

God issued from the Father, but it has come to men through Jesus Christ. The statement is reminiscent of John 1:18: "No man hath seen God at any time; the only begotten Son, which is in the bosom of the Father, he hath declared him."

The reference could be to an actual saying of Jesus, but we need not insist on this interpretation. It is in fact more likely that John was thinking not of any one statement made by Christ, but of the substance of the whole revelation of God communicated through Christ — in what He said, what He did, and what He was in His person.

2. *The reporting of the message* (verse 5). "This then is the message which we . . . declare unto you." The Greek word means "to announce," "report," "bring back tidings." It is used with some degree of frequency in the gospel of John and in the book of Acts, but occurs only in this verse in I John. Some interpreters feel that the word was used especially of authoritative announcements. They cite its use by some secular writers of the proclamations of kings and of the reports of envoys. Moreover, in the Septuagint the term is often used of God's message to and through the prophets. There may be, therefore, at least a suggestion of John's sense of authority.

3. *The substance of the message* (verse 5). "This then is the message . . . *that God is light, and in him is no darkness at all.*" This is an especially emphatic statement. It conveys the thought that God is light essentially; indeed, He is perfect, unmixed light. This stress is brought out by the order of words (Greek, "God light is") and by the use of contrast ("and in him is no darkness at all").

Another device used to strengthen the statement is a double negative, not proper in English but frequently used in Greek to make a statement markedly emphatic. (See Matt. 5:20; Luke 6:37; John 10:28; I Thess. 5:3; *et al.*) The words "at all" in KJV are an attempt to bring out the force of the Greek. Westcott renders it, "Darkness there is not in Him, no, not in any way" (p. 16). All and every kind of darkness is excluded from His nature. "He is light, all light, only light" (Maclaren, p. 248).

John's affirmation about God as light should be studied alongside three other similar declarations in the Johannine writings: "God is Spirit" (John 4:24, ASV); "God is love" (I John 4:8); and God "is true" (I John 5:20). Plummer says "God is Spirit," "God is light," "God is love" "are probably the nearest approach to a definition of God that the human mind could frame or comprehend" (p. 23).

There are at least three interpretations of "light." First, there are those who understand it to refer to *the majesty, the splendor, and the glory of God*. Admittedly, light is an appropriate symbol for these ideas, but it is to be doubted that in this context the statement was primarily intended to teach these things.

The second interpretation takes light to be symbolic of *the moral perfection of God*. As Calvin puts it, "There is nothing in Him but what is bright, pure, and unalloyed" (p. 163). Other commentators state this concept of moral perfection in terms of "absolute holiness," "purity and love and truth," "perfect goodness and beauty," and so forth. This interpretation is in line with the symbolic and moral significance which the Bible often assigns to light and darkness. (See, for instance, the use of "darkness" in 2:8-11. For similar references to "light" as symbolic of righteousness, see Isa. 5:20; Rom. 13:11-14; Eph. 5:8-14, *et al*.)

Others, pointing out that the primary idea in light is illumination, understand the figure to mean that God is *self-revealing*. They explain that as it is the nature of light to shine and to make visible (that is, to communicate itself), so it is the nature of God to reveal Himself, to make Himself known. Law, who argues forcefully for this interpretation, writes that God as light "is always seeking to shine into the minds He has made in His own Image" (p. 60). "God is Light," he concludes, "signifies the inward necessity of the Divine Nature to reveal itself, the fact of its perfect and eternal self-revelation in Christ, and the correlative fact of men's spiritual illumination thereby" (p. 66).

There is an element of truth in each of these interpretations; perhaps they should be combined. The leading thought, however, seems to be that of self-revelation. God has revealed Himself, and in this revelation we learn that He is a God of perfect purity and glorious majesty.

Our interpretation of "and in him is no darkness at all" will be governed by our understanding of "God is light." If "light" be taken as a symbol of moral perfection, then "darkness," its opposite, must be symbolic of moral evil. Understood in this manner, the statement may be an allusion to the gnostic idea that Deity embraced both light and darkness. The supreme God, in their thought, was pure spirit and untainted, but they taught that the final aeon emanating from Him was evil. Against this John asserts that there is nothing in God that has affinity with evil.

On the other hand, if one subscribes to the view that "light" points to the self-revealing character of God, then this statement may be understood as emphasizing the completeness of the divine revelation.

4. *A conclusion* (verses 6-7). Verses 6 and 7 affirm a logical conclusion drawn from the statement that God is light: *If we say that we have fellowship with him, and walk in darkness, we lie, and do not the truth: But if we walk in the light, as he is in the light, we have fellowship one with another, and the blood of Jesus Christ his Son cleanseth us from all sin.* "Worship," writes Maclaren, "is always aspiration after, and conformity to, the character of the god worshipped, and there can be no true communion with a God who is light unless the worshipper walks in light. In plain language, all high-flying pretensions to communion with God must verify themselves by practical righteousness" (p. 249).

"If we say" is a phrase occurring three times in the last half of chapter 1 (verses 6, 8, 10). It introduces three false assertions apparently made by John's gnostic opponents. The first assertion (verse 6) is that sin (walking in darkness) is a matter of no consequence, that it does not in any way affect our fellowship with God. The gnostics held that it was a matter of indifference whether one lived a righteous life; knowledge, to them, was the only thing that mattered. Indeed, it was sometimes urged that to reach the highest form of illumination, men must experience every kind of action, however evil. John strenuously objects.

The form of the conditional statement expresses a probable contingency. Brooke, commenting upon this, observes that throughout the epistle John "writes under a pressing sense of danger. He is not wasting his weapons on purely hypothetical situations" (p. 13).

"Fellowship with him" means fellowship with God the Father. Such fellowship is the highest privilege of Christian faith.

To "walk," a common New Testament metaphor, is used ethically for the walk of life, the whole of one's manner of living (cf. Eph. 4:1). The present tense emphasizes a habitual action. To walk "in darkness" is to "choose and use the darkness as our sphere of action" (Westcott, p. 19).

How one interprets life in the darkness depends upon how he interprets "God is light." Darkness is the absolute opposite of that statement. If light primarily denotes purity, then living in darkness speaks of living an impure life. On the other hand, if light denotes God's self-revelation, then walking in darkness signifies disregard for or defiance of what He has revealed of Himself. That is to say, one who walks in darkness lives his life without reference to the revealed will of God. Either way, to walk in darkness is to live a life of sin.

For the words "we lie, and do not the truth" NEB has "our words and our lives are a lie."

"Truth" may speak of doctrine or of conduct. Here it indicates a way of life, something to be expressed in action, not in theory.

Plummer, commenting on verse 6, writes: "A life in moral darkness can no more have communion with God, than a life in a coal-pit can have communion with the sun."

In verse 7 John gives the positive side of the matter. *But if we walk in the light, as he is in the light, we have fellowship one with another, and the blood of Jesus Christ his Son cleanseth us from all sin.* Walking in the light, in this context, probably denotes a life lived in conformity to the revealed will of God. The Greek word is in the present tense and suggests that this is the habit or the pattern of one's conduct.

Two benefits are mentioned as accruing to those who walk habitually in the light. One is that they have fellowship "one with another." Calvin interprets "one with another" to mean believers' fellowship *with God*. John, he explains, "sets God on one side and us on the other" (p. 164). Spurgeon, who follows Calvin, paraphrases it: "We have mutual fellowship, between God and our souls there is communion" (p. 486). Ronald Knox's translation of the Vulgate conveys the same sense: "God dwells in light; if we too live and move in light, there is fellowship between us." And it is true that, in light of the statement of verse 6, the idea of fellowship with God is what one naturally expects to find repeated here. In spite of this, though, most interpreters think the reference is to *fellowship among Christians.*

The change from one (fellowship with God) to the other (fellowship among Christians) is not as abrupt as might at first appear, for both aspects of our fellowship are intimately bound up together. "A closer walk with God," writes Ramsay, "involves a closer walk with man" (p. 251). Another way of putting it is that fellowship among Christians is both the result and the expression of fellowship with God. On this point Barrett offers a comment worthy of notice: "The communion of saints is an unmistakable proof that the saints themselves are in communion with God; and, on the other hand, the interruption of our personal fellowship with God, dryness and barrenness in prayer, loss of all joy in worship or in praise, are due, far more often than we are apt to believe, to a breach in our fellowship with one another" (p. 48). "The Bible," said Wesley, "knows nothing of a solitary religion."

A second benefit of walking in the light is expressed in the statement that "the blood of Jesus Christ his Son cleanseth us from all sin." The "blood" is a reference to Christ's death considered as a divinely-appointed sacrifice. Its immense significance is expressed in many ways in Scripture. For example, in Mark 14:24 it is that which seals the new covenant between God and men; in Ephesians 1:7 it is the means of our redemption; in Colossians 1:20 it is the means of establishing peace with God; in Hebrews 9:14 it is the instrument by which the conscience is purged from dead works, and so forth.

"Cleanseth from all sin" does not mean that believers are completely freed from sin; it does teach, however, that the blood of Jesus has an efficacy that extends to the whole Christian life. The verb is in the present tense and stresses a continuous and progressive act. Some interpreters see this cleansing as including justification, by which we are made right with God, and sanctification, by which the power of sin in our lives is gradually broken. It is better to understand the statement here in a less inclusive sense, for John is thinking of the effect of the blood upon those who have already been justified, who are (in his words) walking in the light. The thought, then, is that the blood of Christ, applied to our lives by the Holy Spirit, removes sin's defilement and works in us a progressive sanctification.

"All sin," which means "every kind of sin," shows that there is no limit to the efficacy of Christ's sacrificial death when it is applied to the believer.

II. FELLOWSHIP AND CONFESSION (1:8-10)

These verses teach that there can be no fellowship with God apart from confession of sins and the forgiveness and cleansing consequent to that act.

Verse 8, introduced by *If we say that we have no sin,* contains a second false assertion. The first assertion (verse 6) denied that sin estranges us from God; this, the second, goes beyond that, claiming that sin is non-existent as far as we are concerned. The NEB reads it, "If we claim to be sinless." One who could make such a claim obviously has not only a narrow conception of sin but also an inadequate view of the divine law. Make the steeple low enough and any man can jump over it.

There may be an allusion to the gnostic teaching that those initiated into the secrets of their system had no need of forgiveness. John insists that a lack of awareness of personal sin is itself a serious defect. The closer we are to the light of God the more conscious we are of our uncleanness and unworthiness. Witness

Isaiah (6:5), Paul (I Tim. 1:15), Augustine (in his *Confessions*), and Luther, who cried out in agony, "Oh, my sins! my sins!"

The expression "have no sin" seems to be used to mark the inward principle of sin as distinguished from the manifestation of this principle in sinful acts (cf. verse 10).

If we claim to be sinless, writes John, two things follow: First, *we deceive ourselves* (verse 8b). Literally, "we lead ourselves astray." The word suggests serious departure from the right path. The use of the active verb with a reflexive pronoun emphasizes our personal responsibility. This self-deception is "our fault, not our misfortune" (Barrett, p. 58).

Second, if we claim to be sinless *the truth is not in us* (verse 8c). "Truth" could be a reference to Christ (John 14:6), but this is not probable. The reference is rather to the truth of the Gospel. Brooke interprets it here to mean truth as "an inner principle, working from within and moulding a man's inner life" (p. 19).

Mark the significance of "in us." Truth may be all around us, near us, and acknowledged, but when we claim sinlessness we show that it has not penetrated our souls.

The other side of the matter is presented in verse 9: *If we confess our sins, he is faithful and just to forgive us our sins, and to cleanse us from all unrighteousness.* "Confess" literally means "to speak the same thing," that is, "to agree with." So when we confess our sins to God, we say the same thing about ourselves and about our sins that God says. We admit to our guilt. Ramsay thinks there is significance in John's use of the word "confess" rather than "say," the word used in verses 6 and 8. "It is easy to 'say' we have sinned, but to 'confess' sin requires a contrite heart" (p. 253).

The use of the plural "sins" is expressive. We confess our sins — all of them — one by one to God; we make no attempt to deny nor conceal anything, whatever the cost in pain and humiliation.

When such confession of sin is made, God may be counted upon to do two things: (1) "to forgive us our sins," which means that He deals with our guilt and removes it, and (2) "to cleanse us from all unrighteousness," which means that He removes the pollution brought about by our sin. Calvin understands "cleanse" to include the ideas of reformation and renewal.

John mentions God's faithfulness and justice in connection with forgiveness and cleansing. "He is faithful" has reference to His word: He will keep His promise of mercy to the penitent (cf. Heb. 10:23;

11:11). "He is . . . just" has reference to His dealings: He forgives and cleanses in a way commensurate with His righteous character. As Calvin remarks, "God, indeed, forgives freely, but in such a way, that the facility of mercy does not become an enticement to sin" (p. 168). He makes a difference between the penitent (one who confesses) and the impenitent (one who does not confess).

Verse 10 contains a third false assertion (cf. verses 6, 8): *If we say that we have not sinned, we make him a liar, and his word is not in us.* This is really the climax of the three false assertions found in verses 5-10. One could theoretically agree that sin affects fellowship with God (verse 6), could agree that sin exists as a principle within our nature (verse 8), and then deny that he actually had committed sins (verse 10). This ascending scale of error is suggested also in the expressions "we lie" (verse 6), "we deceive ourselves" (verse 8), "we make God a liar" (verse 10).

"Have not sinned" translates a perfect tense, suggesting that the speaker claims to be in a condition of never having committed an act of sin. Such a person, John charges, makes God "a liar" (verse 10b). "This," Barrett remarks, "is the final and most awful result of the denial of sin" (p. 61). Such denial makes God a liar because God's entire plan for the redemption of men is based on the fact of human sin. As Ramsay says, "To claim exemption from sin is to impeach the verdict of God on the human race. If sin be not the fundamental fact in man's present condition, the gospel is irrelevant" (p. 254). Plummer writes: "God's promise to forgive sin to the penitent would be a lie if there were no sin to be repented of. And more than this; God's whole scheme of salvation assumes that all men are sinful and need to be redeemed: therefore those who deny their sinfulness charge God with deliberately framing a vast libel on human nature." Paul's words are a fitting reply to this slander: "Heaven forbid! God must prove true though every man prove a liar!" (TCNT).

Furthermore, John states that if we claim never to have sinned God's "word is not in us" (verse 10c; cf. John 5:38). "His word" might conceivably be taken as a reference to Christ, the personal Word of God; it is better, however, to understand it as a reference to the Gospel (cf. "the truth," verse 8). To say that God's Word is "not in us" is to assert that the Gospel has never found a home in our hearts, that our character and conduct are not shaped by its power. Ross adds, "The delusion against which John is here warning us would be impossible if we steeped our minds in Scripture" (p. 147).

III. FELLOWSHIP AND CHRIST'S ADVOCACY (2:1-2)

These verses teach that fellowship with God is impossible apart from Christ our Advocate. It is He who, in spite of our lapses, maintains our fellowship.

David Smith points up the connection with the preceding discussion. John, he says, was thinking of "the possibility of a twofold perversion of his teaching: (1) 'If we can never in this life be done with sin, why strive after holiness? It is useless; sin is an abiding necessity.' (2) 'If escape be so easy, why dread falling into sin? We may sin with light hearts, since we have the blood of Jesus to cleanse us.' 'No,' he answers, 'I am not writing these things to you either to discourage you in the pursuit of holiness or to embolden you in sinning, but, on the contrary, in order that . . . ye may not sin' " (p. 173). Smith likens the situation to that of a physician who might say to his patient, "Your trouble is obstinate; the poison is in your blood, and it will take a long time to eradicate it. But I do not tell you this to discourage you or make you careless; no, on the contrary, to make you watchful and diligent in the use of the remedy" (p. 173).

We will consider three things in the passage: (1) the address to the readers (verse 1a), (2) the statement of purpose (verse 1b), and (3) the explanation of Christ's advocacy (verses 1c-2).

1. *The address* (verse 1a). Here for the first time John uses an expression which occurs seven times in the epistle (here, 2:12, 13, 18, 28; 3:18; 4:4). Actually, two different terms are rendered *little children,* but the distinction in meaning is only slight. Both are terms of affection, and are commensurate with the tradition that the author was an aged man, looked upon by his readers as their authoritative teacher. The pronoun *my,* used only here to modify "little children," adds to the phrase a peculiarly tender tone.

2. *The statement of purpose* (verse 1b). The apostle's purpose in writing is next stated: *these things write I unto you, that ye sin not* (verse 1b). It is not certain whether "these things" should be understood as a reference to the content of the whole letter or merely to the preceding verses (especially 1:8-10). Brooke argues for the former, but the latter view seems to be more in keeping with the tenor of the passage.

"That ye may not sin" shows that John's purpose in writing was not to condone sin, but to prevent it. The tense of the Greek verb suggests isolated acts of sin rather than a habitual state. It points up that John's object was not simply to secure that the main current of his readers' lives be godly, but that they be kept from committing even a single sin. This, of course, is the ideal.

3. *The explanation of Christ's advocacy* (verses 1c-2). John, quite conscious of the fact that we do not measure up to the ideal, hastens to add, *And if any man sin* — the words imply an act of sin, not a continuous state of sin — *we have an advocate with the Father, Jesus Christ the righteous* (verse 1c). The general sense is that when we lapse into sin Jesus Christ pleads our case in the Father's presence and thus assures our standing before Him.

"Advocate" translates a word which is used only here and in the Upper Room Discourse in John 14-16 (where KJV renders it "Comforter"). Jesus used it of the Holy Spirit (John 14:16, 26; 15:26; 16:7). Here John uses it of Jesus. The two passages complement one another. Here on earth we have the Holy Spirit as our Advocate; in heaven we have Christ as our Advocate.

Interpreted literally, the term suggests one called to another's side to take his part, to plead his cause, or in some other way to give him help. "Advocate," "pleader," "intercessor" — these are all legitimate translations; "advocate," however, is on the whole the best rendering of the word. *The New Berkeley Version* uses "counsel for our defense."

Ramsay reminds us that the language of advocacy is metaphorical and cautions us that "the circumstances of a court of law, which the word suggests, are very far away from the thought of the apostle" (p. 257). Indeed, Christ's advocacy is not a matter of words; it consists in what He is and has done for us. Calvin states it well: "The intercession of Christ is a continual application of his death for our salvation" (p. 171). Ramsay writes similarly: "It is the efficacy of His sacrifice accepted by God which constitutes the Redeemer's plea" (p. 256). So also David Smith: "Our Advocate does not plead that we are innocent or adduce extenuating circumstances. He acknowledges our guilt and presents His vicarious work as the ground of our acquittal" (pp. 173-174).

Four matters are mentioned which point up the fitness of Christ to be our Advocate. One is the uniqueness of His relation to Deity: he is our Advocate "with the Father." The use of the word "Father" rather than "God" calls attention to the Father-Son relationship existing between God and our Advocate. "It is not a stern Judge but a loving Father before whom He has to plead" (Plummer, p. 34). Furthermore, the Greek employs a preposition which may denote a relationship between equals, thus implying that Christ our Advocate enjoys equality with God (cf. John 1:1).

A second factor in Christ's fitness to be our Advocate is His relation to us. Note the human name "Jesus." Bearing our nature, He can plead our case with full knowledge and deep sympathy. (Compare Heb. 4:15.)

A third factor is Christ's own personal sinlessness (cf. Heb. 7:26). He is "Jesus Christ *the righteous.*" As such "He can enter the Presence from which all sin excludes. He needs no advocate for Himself" (Brooke, p. 27). The Greek is so arranged that emphasis is placed on the word for "righteous."

Finally, Christ is uniquely suited to be our Advocate because *he is the propitiation for our sins* (verse 2a). Indeed, if this were not so He could not be our Advocate, for His heavenly ministry on our behalf is based upon His propitiatory death on the cross. Williams' rendering expresses the meaning: "And He is Himself the atoning sacrifice for our sins." The thought is that Christ is both ministering priest and sacrificial victim; He is both propitiator and propitiation.

The word translated "propitiation" is found in the New Testament only here and in I John 4:10, though the corresponding verb is found in Luke 18:13 and Hebrews 2:17. Another word having the same root as the word in our text is found in Romans 3:25 and Hebrews 9:5. The basal idea in all these words is that of appeasing (propitiating) an offended person.

Many interpreters, however, feel that "propitiation" is misleading as a translation for this word group in the New Testament. Propitiation, they say, has overtones of a pagan concept of God. They contend, therefore, that "expiation" is a better word than "propitiation." (Compare RSV, which renders it "means of forgiveness.")

The difference in the two words is essentially this: "Propitiation" has reference to persons; "expiation" has reference to things. *God* is propitiated; *sin* is expiated. In other words, "expiation" suggests the removal of that which offends God; "propitiation" suggests the appeasing of God's anger. In truth, both of these things were done at the cross; the question concerns only the meaning of the Greek word.

C. H. Dodd has championed the idea of expiation. Discussions of it may be found in his commentary on I John as well as in his commentary on Romans. Leon Morris, in *The Apostolic Preaching of the Cross,* has argued very forcefully for the retention of the word "propitiation."

The whole idea of propitiation is lifted out of the realm of pagan thought when we remember that though there was something in the nature of God that demanded propitiation, there was also something in His nature which led Him to provide the propitiation. As Barrett writes, "So far from propitiation and love being irreconcilable, propitiation itself is the work of love" (p. 70).

In the last part of verse 2 John declares that Christ is the propitiation not only for our sins *but also for the sins of the whole world*. The idea must be that Christ is actually the propitiation for the sins of believers; He is potentially the propitiation for the whole world. Obviously, John does not mean to teach that Christ by His death on the cross actually propitiated the sins of the whole world. To understand John as saying this is to understand him as teaching universalism, that all people are saved. This surely was not his idea.

Attention should be called to the fact that the words "the sins of" are in italics in KJV. This means there is no equivalent for them in the Greek. David Smith acknowledges that the KJV rendering is grammatically possible but contends that "it misses the point. There are *sins*, special and occasional, in the believer; there is *sin* in the world; it is sinful through and through. The Apostle means 'for our sins and that mass of sin, the world'. . . . The remedy is commensurate with the malady" (p. 174).

IV. FELLOWSHIP AND OBEDIENCE (2:3-6)

These verses teach that there can be no fellowship apart from obedience to God's commands, that fellowship with God expresses itself in heartful surrender to His will.

John's heretical opponents claimed that knowledge of God freed men from the obligations of the moral law. John teaches that loving obedience to the divine will, far from being optional to the Christian, is the only way we have of proving that we know God. There is nothing, therefore, that can take the place of consistent obedience in heart and conduct. Knowledge of the Bible, orthodox beliefs, formal acts of worship — all of these are nothing if a sincere spirit of obedience is lacking (cf. I Sam 15:22; Jer 7:22 f.).

Obedience to God involves submission to His authority and compliance with His desires and commands. It is both an attitude of heart and a way of life. It is the fruit of faith (Heb. 11:8; Jas. 2:21 ff.) and is nurtured by gratitude (Rom. 12:1 f.).

The word "obey" is not used in the verses before us, but what obedience means is brought out in three expressions: keeping God's commandments (verses 3-4), keeping God's Word (verse 5), and walking as Jesus walked (verse 6).

1. *Keeping God's commandments* (verses 3-4). The essence of this brief paragraph is stated in the third verse: *And hereby we do know that we know him, if we keep his commandments.* The verse teaches three important truths: (1) we can know God; (2) we can know that we know Him; (3) this assurance comes through obedience to His commands.

The word translated "hereby" (literally, "in this") is used frequently in I John. We cannot always be certain whether it points forward to what is about to be written or backward to what has already been written. Here it seems quite clearly to point forward. The NEB brings this out: "Here is the test by which we can make sure that we know him: do we keep his commands?"

"We do know," a present tense verb, denotes a progressive knowledge gained by experience. Here it means something like "we perceive."

The second occurrence of "know" in this verse ("we know him") translates the same word in Greek, but the tense of the word is different. The full thought is "we have come to know and do now know." To "know" God, a favorite concept in John, is to be in fellowship with God.

To "keep" God's commands, which is to be equated with walking in the light (1:7) and not sinning (2:1), speaks of practical conformity to the will of God — both in outward conduct and in inward disposition. The Greek verb means to keep watch over, to be on the watch so as to obey and to fulfill. Thus the keeping of God's commands is not a perfunctory and formal thing. It is a living, watchful observance both of the letter and of the spirit of the divine precepts.

The use of the present tense suggests that keeping God's commands is the pattern of life for the person who truly knows God.

Verse 4, essentially a negative restatement of the thought of verse 3, clearly alludes to those heretical teachers who claimed that obedience is irrelevant to knowledge of God. John insists that nothing could be farther from the truth. With characteristic abruptness he affirms that any person whose claim to know God is not supported by a life of obedience is *a liar.* Moreover, *the truth is not in him.*

"Truth" refers to revealed truth, what God has made known about Himself in Jesus (cf. 1:8). To say that the truth "is not in" a person may mean that it is not an active principle operative in his life (Brooke). Plummer thinks John means that the person so described has lost the ability to recognize truth.

The tense of *keepeth* shows that John was thinking of habitual action. The word translated *commandments* is one of John's favorites, being used approximately fourteen times in this epistle. It is a rather inclusive word as used here, though it may be that John was thinking particularly of the command to love. At any rate, this idea is picked up and developed in greater detail beginning at the seventh verse.

2. *Keeping God's Word* (verse 5). At first sight, this verse seems to be simply a restatement of the thought of verse 3. It should be seen, however, not merely as a restatement, but as an expansion of the earlier verse. As Plummer says, "John's apparent retrogressions are real advances" (p. 38).

No sharp distinction is to be made in the meaning of *his word* (verse 5) and "his commandments" (verses 3, 4). If there is any difference at all, it is that the reference to commandments is more specific and the reference to God's Word is more general. That is to say, "commandments" refers to specific precepts; "his word," which includes the commandments, refers to God's whole revealed will.

Verily is not the word which is translated "verily, verily" in some of the discourses of Jesus. The word employed by Christ called attention to the importance of what He was about to say. John's word stresses reality. It might be rendered "truly," "indeed," or "really."

The love of God may be interpreted in three different ways: man's love for God (RSV), God's love for man (Beck), or a God-kind of love (NEB). Someone has suggested that the indefiniteness of the phrase should be retained in translation, for all three of these ideas are indissolubly connected. If we must choose, the first is to be preferred.

The word translated *hath . . . been perfected* is used four times in this epistle (here, 4:12, 17, 18). (Only Hebrews and the gospel of John use it more frequently.) Its use here does not mean that our love for God is made perfect in the sense of being flawless or all that it should be. Basically, the word means to bring a thing to its proper end, or to bring to fruition. The *New Berkeley Version* renders it, "has . . . reached maturity."

The idea seems to be that when a person keeps God's Word, love (whether God's love for us or ours for Him) achieves its end and object. (Compare Beck's rendering: "But if you do what He

says, God's love has in you really accomplished what He wants.")
Obedience, then, is the proper fruit of love. "If ye love me," said
Jesus, "ye will keep my commandments" (John 14:15, ASV).

Hereby know we that we are in him is understood by some
interpreters as going with what precedes it. Beck, for instance:
"That's how we know we're in Him." (See also KJV.) Most interpreters, however, feel that it is better to take the words with what
follows, that is, as introducing the statement in verse 6. NEB: "Here
is the test by which we can make sure that we are in him: whoever
claims. . . ." (See also RSV, Williams, Berkeley, *et al.*)

To be "in him" is to be in union with Him. The pronoun may
refer either to God or to Christ.

3. *Walking as Jesus walked* (verse 6). Verse 6, though it uses
different language, is a reiteration of the emphasis on obedience
which has been the theme of verses 3-5. Indeed, the discussion of
those verses reaches a climax in this statement. Verse 3 speaks of
"knowing" God; verse 5, of "being in" Him; and verse 6, of "abiding in" Him. One should not, however, make dogmatic distinctions
in the meanings of these terms, for to know God, to be in God, and
to abide in God all have to do with a vital union and fellowship
with Him. However, "abiding in" does stress the habitual character
of the relationship.

Ought expresses moral obligation. Altogether John uses it four
times in his epistles (here; I John 3:16; 4:11; III John 8). Paul uses
it of the husband's obligation to love his wife (Eph. 5:28).

Walk is, of course, used figuratively (cf. 1:6, 7). It is a word
used frequently in this sense in the epistles of Paul and ten times
in this manner in the epistles of John. The word speaks of one's
conduct or the whole round of his life's activities. Thus, to walk
as Jesus walked is to live as Jesus lived—in love, in holiness, in
service, in dependence on the Father, and so forth.

FOR FURTHER STUDY

1. Read articles on "Light," "Sin," "Blood," "Advocate," and
"Propitiation," in a Bible Dictionary. *The Zondervan Pictorial Bible
Dictionary* and *The New Bible Dictionary* are both useful one-vol-
ume dictionaries.

2. Read I John in a translation you have not used before. Mark
and study those passages which relate to the death of Christ or to
the purpose of His coming to earth.

3. Alexander Maclaren has two sermons on the verses treated
in this chapter. Spurgeon has six.

CHAPTER THREE

The Law of Love

(1 John 2:7-17)

John has shown that the keeping of God's commands is the test of real knowledge of God. Now he singles out one specific injunction for special attention. This, the command to love, may be said to include all the others (cf. Matt. 22:36-40; Rom. 13:8 ff.). Because it recurs six times within the five chapters of I John, Findlay calls it *"the* commandment" of the epistle.

John should not be understood in this passage as putting up a straw man. The manner of expression throughout shows that he had in mind specific instances where the command to love was being broken. If our understanding of the background of the letter is correct, we may conclude that the culprits were the gnostics. Arrogant, contemptuous, and exclusive, they were the epitome of an unloving attitude.

This section falls into two divisions. Verses 7-11 relate to love for our brothers; verses 12-17 speak of love for the world. The former we are to practice; the latter we are to avoid.

I. LOVE FOR BROTHER (verses 7-11)

Commandment occurs four times in these verses (three times in verse 7, one time in verse 8). Precisely what command was in mind, we are not told. Some therefore take it as a reference to the charge just given to imitate Christ (2:6). The context, however, favors the view that John was thinking of the command to practice brotherly love. Findlay states it well: " 'The commandment' here intended can be none other than Christ's law of love for His disciples — that which our Lord singled out amongst the Divine precepts to stamp it for His own by saying, 'This is my commandment, that you love one another, as I loved you' (John 15:12)" (p. 155).

John begins with an affectionate address ("Beloved," ASV) which corresponds to the nature of the command he is about to urge upon his readers. The same term is used in five other places in the epistle (3:2, 21; 4:1, 7, 11).

The following points are brought out in reference to the command to love: (1) its oldness (verse 7), (2) its newness (verse 8a), (3) its appropriateness to the Christian era (verse 8b), and (4) its capacity to reveal character (verses 9-11).

1. *Its oldness* (verse 7): *Beloved, no new commandment write I unto you, but an old commandment which ye had from the beginning* (verse 7a, ASV).

By "new" John means novel, new in kind or quality. "Old" suggests that the command under discussion was one with which the readers should have been familiar. It was a prominent feature of the teachings of Jesus and for centuries before the Christian era it lay embedded in the Mosaic law. Indeed, the command to love is, at least in principle, as old as creation, for the law of love is written into the very structure of the world. The Greek word suggests that though given long ago, the command remains in force. "It was old, but not obsolete, ancient, but not antiquated" (Plummer, p. 40).

In verse 7b John explains that his readers had this command "from the beginning." One cannot be sure whether the "beginning" refers to the beginning of the Christian era, the beginning of the readers' instruction in the Gospel, or the beginning of their experience as Christians (cf. 2:24; 3:11; II John 6). It is not really important to decide, for the emphasis seems not to be on a definite starting point as much as on the idea of long continuance. When John wrote, this love command had for years been echoing among the churches. "The real force of the expression is to heighten the contrast of the 'newer' [gnostic] teaching which placed knowledge higher than love" (Brooke, p. 35).

The old commandment, the apostle adds, *is the word which ye heard* (verse 7c, ASV). In describing this commandment as "the word which ye heard," John teaches that the stress on brotherly love is an essential part of the Gospel, not something added to it at a later time. "There were new-fangled speculations and novelties rushing in like a flood; but the apostle recalls them to what has been an essential element of Christianity ever since they and their fathers heard of Christ, to what therefore has stood the test of time" (Ramsay, p. 261).

2. *Its newness* (verse 8a). The second thing which John emphasizes is the newness of the command: *Again, a new commandment I write unto you.* This at first appears to be a contradiction of what was said in the preceding verse, but it really isn't. The key to the matter is the word "again," which here means "in another sense," "from another point of view." Verse 7 teaches that in itself the command to love is not new. Verse 8 teaches that there is, however, another sense in which it is new.

In at least three ways the command is new: First, it is new in its authority. Though the essence of it can be found in the Old Testament, Jesus, as it were, gave it new birth, clothed it with fresh sanction, and enjoined it as the command for the new age which He inaugurated (John 13:34).

Second, it is new in its standard. That is to say, Christ made the command new by making His own love its model (John 13:34). He thereby gave fresh meaning to it.

Third, it is new in practice and application. As Conner says, "It is as old as the Gospel and as new as each soul's experience of the love of God in Christ Jesus" (p. 63). Ramsay explains that though the command is as "old as the earliest apostolic preaching, it is ever new as a fresh and vital and present force. 'Old as the sun, new as the dawn' " (p. 261).

Some interpreters think John was speaking autobiographically. They understand the words to be a sort of confession that though the command had been there all the time the apostle had never adequately understood it. At long last, however, he has been gripped by its power. As a result the fiery, passionate nature of the "son of Thunder" was subdued, and intolerance and self-seeking gave way to gentleness and love. "A touch of sadness haunts the phrase, as though the old apostle confessed a life-long lack and a late discovery" (Blaiklock, p. 17).

Which thing is true in him and in you (verse 8b) teaches that the newness of the command can be seen both in Christ and in believers. Weymouth expresses the sense: "And yet I am writing you a new command, for such it really is, so far as both He and you are concerned." Goodspeed's rendering is similar: "Yet it is a new command that I am writing you; it is newly realized in him and in yourselves."

"Which thing" (translating a neuter word) is a reference not to the command (a feminine word in Greek) but to the idea of its newness. This newness *is true* (that is, actual or real) "in him" (Christ) and "in you" (John's readers). There is significance in the fact that the preposition is repeated both before "him" and before "you." The repetition suggests that the newness of the command is true in the case of Christ in a different sense from that in which it is true in the experience of His people.

Love was new in Christ's case because His life embodied and demonstrated it in a manner never before known. In Him love burst upon the world as a new and startling reality. Love was new in the case of John's readers because it was for them an entirely new way of life. "As a new thing it came to them, and was manifest through them to the world. It brought a new day in the relation of man to man. . . . The world looked on and said, 'Behold how these Christians love one another'" (Conner, p. 64). The command is new in our case as it is repeated and expressed anew in our experience.

3. *Its appropriateness to the new era* (verse 8c). This old, yet new, command corresponds to the new era introduced by the Gospel. This is suggested by John's statement of his reason[1] for urging this command on his readers: *I am writing you . . . because the darkness is passing away, and the true light is already shining* (verse 8c, RSV). The gist of it is that "the ideal state of things, to which the perfect fulfillment of this commandment belongs, has already begun" (Plummer, p. 41).

The use of the present tense verbs is to be noticed. The change from darkness to light is in process; the darkness is not entirely gone, but the true light is already shining. "Darkness," symbolic of sin, ignorance, error, the absence of God, stands for the old order. The "true light" is the light of God's self-revelation, now embodied in Christ (cf. 1:5). It may reflect the statement of John 1:9: "This was the real light, the light that comes into the world and shines on all men" (TEV). This light "shines on in the darkness, and the darkness has never overpowered it" [John 1:5, Weymouth].

The Greek word rendered "true" (not the same as that used earlier in this verse) means "real" or "genuine" as opposed to what

---

[1]Some scholars see this clause not as a statement of John's reason for writing but as a justification for calling the love-command new: It is new because it is a part of a new order.

is counterfeit or spurious. A favorite word with John, it is used twenty-three times in his writings (four times in this epistle) and only five times in the remainder of the New Testament. Its use here marks the contrast between the genuine light of the Gospel (Christ) and the false light of human speculation (especially the gnostic philosophy). In addition, there may be an allusion to "the dim light of the Jewish Law" (Smith, p. 176).

4. *Its capacity to reveal character* (verses 9-11). One's response to the command to love reveals his essential character. In short, the man who habitually breaks that commandment shows that he belongs to the darkness; the man who habitually keeps it shows that he belongs to the light. John puts it like this: *He that saith he is in the light and hateth his brother, is in the darkness even until now. He that loveth his brother abideth in the light* (verses 9-10a, ASV).

"He that saith" points up that John was thinking of an actual case of gross inconsistency between profession and conduct. "These spiritual boasters," writes Ramsay, "made everything of their enlightenment and nothing of their life" (p. 262). This is the fifth time John has explicitly referred to them (1:6, 8, 10; 2:4).

To claim to be "in the light" is to claim to be regenerate, to be in that realm over which the light of God's self-revelation sheds its radiant beam.

"Hateth," a present tense, denotes one for whom hatred is a fixed and settled principle of life. "Loveth," another present tense, denotes one for whom love is a fixed and settled principle of life.

It is instructive to see what John says about these two radically different people — the man who hates and the man who loves. The former is described in verses 9 and 11; the latter, in verse 10.

Three things are said about the man who hates: First, he exists "in the darkness even until now" (verse 9b, ASV). That is to say, darkness is the moral and spiritual atmosphere of his life, in spite of the fact that the true light is shining in the world. He is "in" the darkness in the sense that he is united with it and a part of it.

"Even until now," somewhat emphatic in Greek, shows that the man who hates, in spite of the fact that he may have an outward connection with the Christian community, has never really left the darkness. He is in the darkness now, and always has been. The light is shining, but he has not seen it.

Second, not only is the man who hates his brother *in* the darkness, he also *walketh in darkness* (verse 11a). That is to say, all of his movements are those of a man groping in the dark. "There is not the firm tread, the confidence, the decision, the ease, the clearness of view, the straightness of course, of one who walks in the light of day. The groping, blind man is his picture" (Sawtelle, p. 20).

To "be" in the darkness is an idea connoting existence and character; to "walk" in the darkness suggests action and conduct. The two things go together. If a man *walks* in the darkness, it is because he *is* in the darkness. "His conduct matches his character; he cannot act otherwise than he is, or walk in any region other than that where his habitation lies" (Findlay, p. 160).

Third, the brother-hater is without direction or goal in life. He *knoweth not whither he goeth* (verse 11c). The main idea of these words is that hatred so perverts a man's every endeavor that it is not possible for him to make conscious progress toward any satisfying goal. His whole life is a blackout. There may be the added suggestion here that the hate-filled man's destiny is itself one of darkness. He rushes headlong into moral and spiritual night, not knowing he is headed for a precipice which will plunge him into the outer darkness of eternal ruin (cf. Prov. 4:18-19).

This man does not know where he is going *because the darkness hath blinded his eyes* (verse 11c, ASV). Like the mole, like the ponies used in coal mines, like the fish of Mammoth Cave, dwellers in darkness eventually lose the ability to appreciate light. "The penalty of living in the darkness is not merely that one does not see, but that one goes blind" (Smith, p. 176). Hatred robs us of all spiritual insight. It blinds us to the virtues of others, the faults in ourselves, and the peril which awaits us if we persist in this course of life.

The case of the true Christian — the man for whom brother-love is a pattern of love — is otherwise. Two things are said about him: One, he *abideth in the light* (verse 10a). That is, he lives or remains in the light of divine revelation. The emphasis is on the word "abideth." "He who loves his brother is always in the Light" (TCNT). The NEB, however, brings out a slightly different stress: "Only the man who loves his brother dwells in light."

Two, because he does live in the light there is *none occasion of stumbling in him* (verse 10b). This clause may be interpreted in either of two ways. "Occasion of stumbling" may, for instance, refer to that which causes the man himself to stumble. The TCNT takes it this way: "there is nothing within him to cause him to stumble." A variation of this is given by NEB ("there is nothing to make him stumble"), David Smith ("there is . . . nothing to trip him up and make him fall"), and Moffatt ("in the light there is no pitfall"). (Compare John 11:9-10.)

Another way of looking at it is to see "occasion of stumbling" as that which causes others to stumble. Goodspeed's rendering brings out this meaning: he "puts no hindrance in anyone's way." So also Williams ("he is no hindrance to others") and TEV ("he has nothing in himself that will cause someone else to sin"). "Want of love," it has been said, "is the most prolific cause of offences."

II. LOVE FOR THE WORLD (verses 12-17)

In the first part of this chapter John has detailed what the Christian is to do: exhibit a spirit of penitence, walk after the example of Christ, and love the brotherhood. This passage, in contrast to the positive teaching of what has gone before, tells what the believer is not to do. The essence of it is the avoidance of the spirit of the world.

There are three clearly marked divisions. Verses 12-14 form a kind of prelude or introduction and give the basis for John's appeal. Verse 15a gives the substance of the appeal. Verses 15b-17 are an expansion of the appeal.

1. *The basis for the appeal* (verses 12-14). Verses 12-14 are not closely related either to what has preceded or to what follows. Law says they are "thrust like a wedge into the middle of a paragraph, separating the positive exposition of the Law of Love (2: 7-11) from the negative (2:14-17)" (p. 306). With a measure of hesitation we are construing the passage with what follows, seeing it as setting forth the basis of the appeal which is given in verses 15-17.

It contains a sixfold statement of the author's reasons for writing. In effect, however, these six statements all point up one thing, namely, that John's impulse to write does not spring from doubt of his readers' Christian experience but from his confidence in it. As Blaiklock writes, "The apostle is about to make a searching and exacting claim, and pauses before he makes it to assure all in his congregation that he addresses them, not as worldlings, but as convinced and victorious Christians" (p. 22).

The structure of the paragraph is somewhat unusual. There are two series or sequences of statements, each containing three reasons for writing. In ASV they read as follows:

¹² I write unto you, my little children, because your sins are forgiven you for his name's sake.

¹³ I write unto you, fathers, because ye know him who is from the beginning.

¹³ I write unto you, young men, because ye have overcome the evil one.

¹³ I have written unto you, little children, because ye know the Father.

¹⁴ I have written unto you, fathers, because ye know him who is from the beginning.

¹⁴ I have written unto you, young men, because ye are strong, and the word of God abideth in you, and ye have overcome the evil one.

Probably the first thing one notices is the repetition of the word "write." Three times John says "I write"; three times he says "I have written." In the Greek the first three statements are translations of the present tense; the last three statements are translations of the aorist tense.

These variations have been explained in different ways. David Smith, for instance, who thinks this epistle was a covering letter for the gospel, understands the present tenses ("I write") as referring to this epistle. The aorist tenses ("I have written") are interpreted as references to the gospel.

Robert Law suggests another explanation. He thinks that after writing verses 12-13b (in which the present tense ["I write"] occurs) John was interrupted; then, after some delay, the apostle came back to complete his epistle and resumed the line of thought by repeating in essence what he had already written in verses 12-13b. Law concludes that the change of tense from present to past (aorist) simply reflects the author's changed point of view.

Others look upon the variation in tense simply as a stylistic device to give emphasis to the statement. The three present tenses ("I write") mean essentially the same thing as the three aorist tenses ("I have written"). In this view the aorist is what the grammarians call "epistolary" and may be translated into English by a present tense. (See TEV.)

Another interesting feature of these verses is the use of three different terms of address. The first statement of each series begins with a reference to the readers as "little children" (verses 12, 13c). (Two different Greek words are used [*teknia,* verse 12; *paidia,* verse 13c], but there seems to be no essential distinction in their meanings here. Both are used as terms of endearment.) In the second statement of each series, John addresses his readers as "fathers"; and in the third statement of each series, he addresses them as "young men."

It is tempting at first to take these three terms as denoting three classes (age groups) of Christians. But if that is what John had in mind, the order is somewhat unnatural. In that case we should have expected "children, young men, fathers," not "children, fathers, young men." Accordingly, it is more likely that by "little children" John was describing all of his readers. We know that elsewhere in the epistle he uses the word like this (2:1, 18, 28; 3:7; 5:21), and it was an especially fitting way for an older man to address those of a younger generation.

After naming all of his readers as his "little children," John subdivides them into two groups: "fathers," referring to the older, more mature members of the congregation; and "young men," embracing all of those who were younger believers. The three expressions then are equivalent to "my children in Christ, old and young."

Conner wisely cautions us not to make distinctions that are too rigid. He points out that the qualities ascribed to the "fathers" and "young men" are about as general as those ascribed to the "little children."

In addition to the terms of address used, it is also instructive to observe the characteristics ascribed to each group. The principal ideas are forgiveness, knowledge of God, and victory over evil.

The readers generally ("little children") are described first as having their sins *forgiven* (verse 12). The verb translates a perfect tense, pointing up that their sins were forgiven at some time in the past and emphasizing that they remain forgiven. Forgiveness naturally stands first in this listing, for it is the fundamental experience of the Christian life and the absolute condition of fellowship with God.

Their sins, John explains, have been forgiven *for his* [Christ's] *name's sake* (verse 12). In Scripture, the name of a person stands for the person's revealed or manifested character. Thus, to believe in the name of Christ is to believe in Christ Himself as He is revealed to us in the Gospel. And to be forgiven "for his name's sake" is to be forgiven on the basis of what Christ is and has done for us.

In addition to the forgiveness which they have experienced, the apostle asserts that all of the Asian Christians (his "little children") have come to know (a perfect tense) *the Father* (verse 13c). That is to say, they have come to know God in His character as Father. The sense of divine sonship seems to be the point of emphasis.

The older believers ("fathers") are especially distinguished by their knowledge: *Ye have known him that is from the beginning* (verses 13a, 14a). The verb translated "have known" must speak in this context of a long and ever-deepening experience. Charles Spurgeon tells of a time when, as a very young man, he was preaching on the faithfulness of God. His aged grandfather, who was sitting behind the young preacher, came forward at one point and said, "My grandson can tell you that, but I can bear witness to it. I have passed my three score years and ten, but still He has been faithful and true" (p. 479). This is the knowledge of which John was speaking — a knowledge which comes by walking with God through the varied experiences of life. Prayer, the study of the Word, devoted service, obedient living — these are for all of us avenues to this deeper knowledge.

"Him who is from the beginning" (ASV) may be a reference to God the Father, but in light of 1:1 it is better to see in the words a reference to Christ as the Eternal One.

Younger believers ("young men"), with whom we often associate fierce moral struggles, are characterized by their spiritual vigor and conquest. They are said to be *strong* (verse 14) and to have the Word of God abiding in them. Twice they are said to have *overcome the wicked one* (verses 13, 14). This latter statement may have primary reference to a victory gained over the teachers of error who were threatening the fellowship of John's readers, a victory which probably led to the withdrawal of those heretics from the Christian company. The statement, however, must not be limited to this, for John speaks elsewhere in more general terms about the believer's victory over evil (5:4-5; cf. 3:6-9).

Confidence of victory, a note found in all of John's writings, is here stated in the strongest possible language. Indeed, John asserts that victory has already been achieved by his readers, for "overcome" translates a perfect tense, denoting that they have conquered the evil one and remain victorious over him. In 5:4-5 it is affirmed that the Christian's faith is that which gives him victory. Here (verse 14) John suggests that one factor in his readers' victory is the abiding within them of the *word of God* (the gospel message). Bunyan's description of Christian's conflict with Apollyon forms a good commentary on the matter.

To speak of the Word as "abiding in" the readers is to suggest that it was a living force permanently active within them. The TEV renders it, "the word of God lives in you"; Norlie, "God's Word is treasured in your hearts"; Phillips, "you have a hold on God's truth." Ramsay writes: "The man whose mind is stored with right principles and true conviction is clad in triple steel" (p. 267).

In the verses immediately following John will remind his readers of their continuing struggle with the world. Here he assures them that they are well-equipped for it. They have been given divine strength, they have the Word of God within them, and they have the confidence born of victories already won against the enemy.

2. *The substance of the appeal* (verse 15a). John states his appeal in terse language: *Love not the world, neither the things that are in the world.* The general import of the words is clear, but popular thinking about the world and worldliness may obscure the meaning which John's readers found here.

"The world" is a term employed by John more often than by all the other New Testament writers put together — seventy-nine times in the gospel and twenty-three times in this epistle. It has at least three different significations in the Johannine writings: (1) It is used of the world of nature, the created order, the material universe (John 1:10; I John 4:17). This world, with its changing seasons, majestic mountains, restless seas, and verdant fields, is a thing of beauty and is to be acknowledged as such by Christians (cf. Psalms 8, 19, *et al.*). (2) It is used of the whole human race thought of as a world fallen into sin and in need of redemption. This world God loves (John 3:16); He feels its burdens and is sensitive to its needs (I John 2:2; 4:9). (3) It is used of unbelieving, pagan society thought of as a rebel order embodying the influences and forces hostile to God (I John 5:19; John 14:30; 15:18, 19; 16:30; cf. James 1:27; 4:4). John saw this world ranged in opposition to the people of God and threatening their very existence on the earth. It is this world which the Christian is not to love.

Findlay explains that the world in this last sense "is not made up of so many outward objects that can be specified; it is the sum of those influences emanating from men and things around us, which draw us away from God. It is the awful down-dragging current in life" (p. 199). Law defines it as "the social organism of evil" (p. 148); Erdman calls it "the society of the unspiritual and the godless" (p. 123); Conner interprets it as "an all-pervasive atmosphere" (p. 81); Dodd takes it to mean "human society as organized under the power of evil" (p. 39); Blaiklock sees it as "almost the 'darkness' of John's earlier theme" (p. 23). The NEB uses the term "godless world."

Blaiklock points out that in our modern western society " 'the world' is a gentler but no less deadly force. It still envelopes the Christian with the subtlety of its attraction and appeal. It is not a menace backed by a hostile, persecuting state, but it is still a facet of man's rebellion, a thrust and urge toward conformity, surrender to the secular multitude, and the death of finer things which is involved in that capitulation" (p. 24).

What does it mean to "love" the world? To answer this question, one must bear in mind what has already been said about the significance of the word "world." To love the world of men, as God loves it, is to demonstrate benevolent, sacrificial good will toward men lost in sin. This is the duty of every Christian. But to love the world as a moral order hostile to God is an altogether different thing. It is to court the world's favor, follow its customs, adopt its ideals, covet its prizes, and seek its fellowship. Loving the world in this sense means setting one's affection on evil and is tantamount to deserting God. This the Christian must not do.

"The things that are in the world" are its lusts, its ambitions, its pleasures, its dominating principles and motives — in a word, those elements in society which stamp it as evil. John summarizes these things in verse 16: "the lust of the flesh and the lust of the eyes and the vainglory of life" (ASV).

3. *The expansion of the appeal* (verses 15b-17). In developing his appeal John gives two reasons for not loving the world. One is that love for the world excludes love for God: *If any man love the world, the love of the Father is not in him* (verse 15b). The TCNT: "When any one loves the world, there is no love for the Father in him." The use of a present tense verb makes clear that John was thinking of love for the world and love for God as ruling principles of life. As such they are mutually exclusive; where one is the other cannot be.

Verse 16 tells why love for God and love for the world are incompatible: *For all that is in the world, the lust of the flesh, and the lust of the eyes, and the pride of life, is not of the Father, but is of the world.* The gist of it is that God and the world belong to two separate spheres. "All that is in the world" is totally different from and directly antagonistic to all that is "of the Father." He lays down one plan or program of life for His people: the world proposes another, which is its antithesis. There can be no compromise.

"All that is in the world," which picks up "the world" (verse 15) and "the things that are in the world" (verse 15), may be translated "all that the world can offer" (TCNT). This is defined as "the lust of the flesh," "the lust of the eyes," and "the pride of life." This "trinity of evil" is literally all that the world has to offer. It is not in its power to give anything nobler or better.

In "the lust of the flesh" the word "flesh" stands for human nature as corrupted by sin. Williams translates it "the lower nature." Barclay calls it "that part of our nature which . . . offers a bridge-head to sin" (p. 68). The "lust" of the flesh means the unlawful desire produced by that nature. The phrase includes all those desires and appetites centered in man's physical nature and exercised without regard to the will of God. The one word "sensuality" describes it.

"The lust of the eyes" speaks of the unlawful craving for that which entices our eyes. Ramsay interprets it of heathen entertainment — "all delight in immoral scenes, spectacles, plays" — and explains that the phrase "needed no commentary for readers familiar with the foul and cruel exhibitions of the circus and the amphitheatre" (p. 268). Dodd, who speaks of it as "the tendency to be captivated by the outward show of things" (p. 41), seems to equate it with materialism. Law thinks that the most obvious example of it is covetousness, but he concludes that the phrase is broad enough to include every kind of unlawful desire which makes its appeal to the eye.

The Greek for "the pride of life" may be translated "the vainglory of life" (ASV), "the proud display of life" (Moffatt), or "the proud pretentions of life" (Williams). Perhaps it means something like pride in, or a pompous display of, material wealth and worldly advantages. It implies an arrogant spirit of self-sufficiency and a vain sense of security, both of which are based upon a false estimate of the stability and value of worldly things.

The Greek words for "pride" and "life" are both worthy of notice. The latter translates a term (*bios*) used by John only here and in 3:17. In both places it denotes the means of supporting life and may be translated "livelihood" or "possessions." (Compare Luke 15:12, "And he divided unto them his *living.*")

"Pride," translating a word used elsewhere in the New Testament only in James 4:16, suggests arrogant display. In earlier Greek it meant "swagger" or "braggadocio." Vincent defines it as "an insolent and vain assurance in one's own resources, or in the stability of earthly things, which issues in a contempt for divine laws" (p. 376).

In saying that these things — sensuality, materialism, and arrogant self-sufficiency — are "not of the Father" John means that they do not originate in God, show no likeness to His character, and are contrary to the life which He wills for His people. "Of the world" means that they come from and belong to that realm which is unalterably opposed to God. They are therefore completely alien to His will. The Christian has no alternative but to flee from them.

A second reason for not loving the world is found in its transitoriness. This is hinted at in verse 16 but is brought out clearly in verse 17a: *And the world passeth away, and the lust thereof.* Williams gives a better rendering: "the world is passing away and with it the evil longings it incites." The use of the continuous present tense ("is passing away") points up that the process of dissolution is already at work.

We must not interpret this as a reference to the destruction of the material universe. "The world" must here, as above in verse 15, be thought of in moral and spiritual terms. It is the world as a rebel order, the world as an organized system marked by hostility to God. It is pagan society, "the whole world" which "lieth in the evil one" (5:19, ASV).

"The lust thereof" may be understood as lust *for* the world, as lust which the world *stimulates* (see Williams' rendering), or simply as the lust or desire *belonging to the world.* There is an obvious allusion to the sinful tendencies mentioned in verse 16.

In writing that the world and "all its allurements (NEB) is passing away" John teaches that human society in its hostility to God has in it the seeds of death, and its final dissolution is certain. Because of this "the world" can give no permanent satisfaction. As an object of desire and affection it is evanescent, vain, and disappointing. To build one's life around it is therefore not only sinful, it is also foolish. It is to bind oneself to a doomed and dying order.

Over against the impermanence of the world and its lust John sets the man whose life conforms to the divine plan: *He that doeth the will of God abideth for ever* (verse 17b). The statement is an assurance of the believer's victory over the world. Williams translates it, "He who perseveres in doing God's will lives on forever." Such a person shares the very life of God and in so doing links himself with eternity.

Join thy heart to the eternity of God, and thou shalt be eternal with Him. — Augustine

FOR FURTHER STUDY

1. Compare what is said about love in I John 2:7-11 with what is recorded in John's gospel, chapters 13 through 16.

2. Make a list of the characteristics or achievements ascribed to "fathers," "young men," etc. in I John 2:12-14.

3. Mark and study the passages in I John in which the readers are addressed as "little children."

4. Make a list of the passages in I John in which the word "world" is used. Read the article on "World" in *The Zondervan Pictorial Bible Dictionary*.

5. Compare I John 2:15 with Romans 12:2 and James 4:4.

CHAPTER FOUR

The Conflict of Truth and Falsehood

(1 John 2:18-28)

I. The Last Hour (18)
II. The Antichrists (19-26)
    1. Their relation to the people of God (19)
    2. Their distinctive beliefs (22-23)
    3. Their evil purpose (26)
III. The Believers' Security (20-28)
    1. Their anointing (20-21, 27)
    2. Their adherence to the Christian message (24-25)
    3. Their union with Christ (27b-28)

To this point in our epistle there has been a mingling of instruction, warning, and assurance. The instruction has concerned the apostolic message, the character and conditions of fellowship, and the meaning and implications of love. The warning has been directed against profession without practice and against the world's deadening influence. Assurance has been given of the true believer's fellowship with God and of his victory over the world.

In the present passage there is that same triple strand of instruction, warning, and assurance. The instruction mainly concerns the Christian's relation to God and truth. The warning is against an insidious error propagated by false teachers. The assurance concerns the validity of the Christian experience of John's readers.

It is in this section (and in the similar teaching of 4:1-6) that the crisis which called forth this letter comes into clearest view. The lines are sharply drawn between truth and falsehood, Christ and antichrist, confession of Christ and denial of Christ, those who have an anointing from the Holy One (true Christians) and those who do not (pretenders).

This passage, like most of I John, defies a logical analysis. Its teaching, however, focuses about three key conceptions. These are

(1) "the last hour," (2) the "many antichrists," and (3) the believer's security against error.

I. THE LAST HOUR (verse 18)

Little children, it is the last hour: and as ye heard that antichrist cometh, even now have there arisen many antichrists; whereby we know that it is the last hour (ASV). "Little children," a characteristic address in I John, is a term of affection suggesting the author's fatherly authority over his readers. Its use here served to enlist their sympathetic interest. It may also have betokened the gravity of the topic about to be discussed.

The affirmation that "it is the last hour" has been the occasion of much controversy. Of the many interpretations which have been proposed, only three seem to be worthy of mention:

First, that the last hour means the period immediately preceding the end of the world. Those who hold this view assert that John felt he was living at the end of the ages, that his day was the immediate prelude to the consummation of world history. Compare Weymouth: "Dear children, the last hour has come." TEV: "My children, the end is near!" This is the position of Dodd, Ramsay, Barclay, and others.

It must be admitted that this interpretation brings out the simplest and most obvious meaning of the words. In like manner, it links up naturally with the context, particularly the statement of verse 17 that "the world is passing away." Observe also that the last reference of this section is to Christ's coming (verse 28).

The principal problem in accepting this explanation is that it seems to involve John in error, for nearly two thousand years have passed and still the end has not come. Too, it seems a bit unlikely that the beloved disciple would lay claim to a knowledge which was admittedly denied to his Lord (Mark 13:32).

Second, that the last hour is a reference to the entire Christian era — that is, the time between Christ's first advent and His return. Norlie's rendering reflects this interpretation: "My children, it is the final age of the world." The proponents of this view point to other passages which use similar language. For example, I Peter 1:20, where it is said that Christ was foreknown before the foundation of the world but was manifested "in this last period of time" (NEB). There is a sense, therefore, in which the world has been in its final stage ever since God became incarnate in Jesus. See also Acts 2: 16-17a; Hebrews 1:2 (NEB). This is the position of Calvin and others.

A telling argument against this interpretation is John's statement that the presence of antichrists is the evidence "whereby we know that it is the last hour" (ASV). The new age was created by the advent of Christ, not by the appearance of antichrists.

Third, that the last hour merely characterizes the Johannine period as a time of crisis. Those who argue for this interpretation see the phrase as marking "the general character of the period and not its specific relation to 'the end' " (Westcott, p. 69). They point out that the Greek text does not have an article before "last hour" and that it should therefore be translated "a last hour," not "the last hour." The meaning then is that John and his readers were living in a perilous hour, a time of extremity, a period exhibiting the distinctive traits of the final hour. Orr speaks of it as *"an eschatological hour,* electric with movements of the unseen principalities which might burst into sight at any time." Then he comments: "Even from our point of time, John's assessment was correct. There are periods when the End draws obviously near, though in course of time the crisis subsides and recedes. The periods of the rise of Islam, the Reformation, the Napoleonic Wars, and the present age, are examples of epochs heavy with destiny" (p. 613).

The chief weakness of this interpretation is that it makes too much of the absence of the Greek article before "last hour." It should be remembered that the definiteness of a Greek word or phrase was not in every case dependent upon the presence of the article. Another qualifying word (such as the adjective "last" in this passage) might make a term quite definite. Furthermore, frequent usage of a word or phrase tended to establish a meaning so fixed that an article was not required for definiteness. Compare such passages as II Timothy 3:1; James 5:3; and I Peter 1:5. These do not have the Greek article, but English versions consistently (and correctly) employ the definite article in each of them. And for what it is worth, a random check of eighteen different translations of the present passage reveals that all eighteen use "the" in rendering this phrase into English.

There is something to be said for each of these interpretations; likewise, no one of them is without its problems. I am inclined to adopt, with slight modification, the first interpretation and to conclude that "the last hour" has been prolonged far beyond what John could have imagined. In light of the reference to the world's "passing away" (verse 17) the assertion here may mean about what is meant when we say that "time is running out." Such a statement would

seem to fall short of a dogmatic affirmation by the apostle that his
day was the immediate prelude to the consummation of the age.

II. THE ANTICHRISTS (verses 19-26)

John found evidence that the period in which he was writing
was the last hour in the prevalence of unbelief and opposition to
Christ: *As ye heard that antichrist cometh, even now have there
arisen many antichrists; whereby we know that it is the last hour*
(verse 18b, ASV). Note "the antichrist" (singular) and "many antichrists." The former "cometh"; the latter "have already arisen"
(TCNT). The singular refers to one personal embodiment of evil to
be manifested at the end of the age. The plural refers to those who,
even as early as John's day, embodied the antichristian spirit and
were in a sense forerunners of the eschatological antichrist.

The word "antichrist" is used in the New Testament only by
John (I John 2:18, 22; 4:3; and II John 7). It may mean either
one who stands against Christ or one who stands in stead of Christ
(that is, takes His place). Law, who contends that the two meanings are to be combined, explains that the Greek preposition *anti,*
when prefixed to another word, denoted "not opposition simply, but
opposition in the guise of similarity" (p. 321). "Antichrist" then
suggests one who, assuming the guise of Christ, opposes Christ. He
is both a counterfeit Christ and a rival Christ, a usurper and an
adversary.

Though John alone uses "antichrist," similar terms are found
elsewhere in the New Testament. In Mark 13:22, for instance, Jesus
is quoted as predicting the coming of "false Christs" and "false
prophets." And Paul, in II Thessalonians 2 tells of a "falling away"
which must come and of a "man of sin" to be revealed before the
coming of the day of the Lord. This man of sin is "the son of
perdition" and opposes and exalts himself "against all that is called
God or that is worshipped." He sits in the temple of God and sets
himself forth as God. His coming is "according to the working of
Satan," but the Lord Jesus "shall slay" him "with the breath of his
mouth" and bring him to nought "by the manifestation of his coming."

We may conclude that Paul's "man of sin" and John's "antichrist" are references to the same eschatological person.

That John could introduce this word without further explanation is an indication that the concept of antichrist was familiar to his
readers. For them, as for Christians generally in the apostolic period,

it was a staple of eschatological belief that there would be a resurgence of evil preceding the Second Coming of Christ. In the post-apostolic age writers like Justin Martyr, Irenaeus, Tertullian, and Jerome dealt frequently with the subject.

The "many antichrists" are to be identified with the heretical teachers whose activity threatened the fellowship of the Asian Christians and occasioned the writing of this letter. Judging from what is said about them here and from what we learn of ancient heresies through non-biblical writings, it seems certain that these errorists had embraced some form of Gnosticism. (See Introduction.)

Three things are asserted of the antichrists in this passage. The first concerns their relation to the people of God (verse 19); the second concerns their distinctive beliefs (verses 22-23); and the third concerns the purpose and aim of their action (verse 26).

1. *Their relation to the people of God* (verse 19). John teaches that the antichrists *went out from us*. From this we conclude that they had had some previous connection with the Christian movement; at one time they claimed to be Christians, were numbered among the godly. But John hastens to make clear that those who seceded from the Christian company were never really a part of the Christian fellowship: "They went out from us, *but they were not of us.*" That is to say, their membership in the Church was outward and formal, not real and vital. They were not true believers; they were only nominal believers. This is plainly expressed by Goodspeed: "They have gone out from our number, but they did not really belong to us." Knox's rendering is similar: "They came of our company, but they never belonged to our company."

John interpreted their failure to persevere as evidence of their want of real faith: *for if they had been of us, they would no doubt have continued with us* (verse 19b). Moffatt puts it, "Had they belonged to us, they would have remained with us." Continuance to the end is the mark of real discipleship (cf. Matt. 10:22; John 8:31). One's failure to continue proves the falsity of his profession.

B. H. Carroll used to say, "When you see a 'star' fall you can know it is not a star." In light of John's statement one could say, "When you see a 'Christian' fall you can know he is not a Christian."

In verse 19c John teaches that the departure of the antichrists from the Christian community was actually the outworking of a divine plan: *but they went out, that they might be made manifest that they were not all of us.* The rendering of TCNT is more perspicuous: "They left us that it might be made clear that they do not, any of them, belong to us." NEB has ". . . so that it might be clear that not all in our company truly belong to it." Their lack of kinship with the people of God had always existed, but their separation brought it to light.

These words, of course, present the matter from the divine point of view. From their own point of view the heretics went out from the church because they were dissatisfied with what they found there. They had no taste for what true believers confessed and lived by, and they went out that they might follow their own peculiar beliefs.

John, from a higher perspective, saw their departure as providential. By leaving the Christian fellowship the heretics unwittingly fulfilled a purpose of God. That purpose was that they be seen in their true character and that thereby their opportunity for damaging the church be limited. Painful though it must have been for the fellowship of believers, the secession of the antichrists was in reality a benefit to them. The threat which they now posed for the people of God was far less dangerous than it would have been had they continued formally as a part of the Christian group.

2. *Their distinctive beliefs* (verses 22-23). Everything was at stake in John's conflict with the antichrists, for their teachings amounted to a repudiation of the whole Gospel. The intensity of the apostle's feeling on this matter is revealed in the opening words of verse 22: *Who is the liar but he that denieth that Jesus is the Christ?* (ASV). The use of the definite article before "liar" suggests that anyone affirming that Jesus is not the Christ is an arch liar. If such a person is not a liar, John seems to say, then there are no liars.

The master falsehood then is the denial "that Jesus is the Christ" (cf. 4:3). The reference is to the distinction which the antichrists made between the man Jesus and the divine Christ. Jesus, in their thinking, was a mere man, begotten through normal reproductive processes and marked by the imperfections common to the human race. The Christ spirit, an emanation from Deity, descended upon Him at His baptism but withdrew from Him just before He died. The historical Jesus, therefore, was not identical with the Christ.

This heresy, the apostle teaches, carries with it two serious consequences. First, the denial that Jesus is the Christ results in a denial of the Father-Son relationship within the Godhead: "Who is the liar but he who denies that Jesus is the Christ? *This is the antichrist, he who denies the Father and the Son"* (verse 22, RSV [italics mine]). The arrangement of the two parts of the verse suggests that in Johannine thought affirming that Jesus is the Christ is the same as affirming that He is the eternal Son of God. Therefore, if Jesus is not the Christ (in the full Johannine sense) then God is not Father and Jesus is not His Son.

Second, to deny that Jesus is the Christ, the Son of God, is to deprive oneself of God as Father: *Whosoever denieth the Son, the same hath not the Father* (verse 23a). This is because Christ is the One who reveals the Father (Matt. 11:27) and affords our only access to the Father (John 14:6). It follows then that those who deny the full deity and the real humanity of Jesus Christ, as do some so-called Christian theologians, are cut off from God. As Meyer says, "The God of those who deny the Son is not the true God, but a false image of their own thoughts, an idol" (p. 537). Ross adds that "the man who denies the Son . . . is an orphan, a fatherless child in the vast loneliness of the universe" (p. 173).

Verse 23b teaches that the only way men can have the Father is by confessing Jesus as His Son. *"He that confesseth the Son hath the Father also"* (ASV).[1] To "confess" the Son is to acknowledge Him (KJV, NEB) or to accept him (TEV) as Son of God. It is the very opposite of "deny," which basically means to reject or disown.

3. *Their evil purpose* (verse 26). The intention of the heretics was to seduce the people of God from the truth. This is stated in verse 26: *These things have I written unto you concerning them that seduce you.* NEB, giving a slightly different turn to it, reads: "So much for those who would mislead you."

"Them that seduce," a present tense participle in Greek, indicates that seduction was an occupation with John's opponents. The thought is repeated in II John 7, where the apostle uses the substantive "deceivers" or "impostors" (TCNT) as a designation for them. Here, the participial phrase with its object may be rendered "those who are trying to mislead you" (TCNT), "those who would deceive you" (RSV), or "those who would lead you astray" (ASV). Observe that each of these translations brings out the idea that the antichrists were not successful in their attempts to deceive true believers.

III. THE BELIEVERS' SECURITY (verses 20-28)

True believers are not at the mercy of antichristian teachers. They have a threefold security: (1) their anointing from the Holy

---

[1]The second half of verse 23 is printed in italics in KJV, indicating that the words have no equivalent in Greek. But they are found in the best Greek manuscripts and are undoubtedly genuine.

One, (2) their adherence to the Christian message, and (3) their union with Christ. We shall consider what John teaches concerning each of these.

1. *Their anointing* (verses 20-21, 27). In an earlier passage (2:1) John assured his readers that they had an Advocate. Here they are told of another priceless spiritual possession — a divine anointing. This anointing is first mentioned in verse 20: *But ye have an unction from the Holy One, and ye know all things.* The idea is repeated in verse 27: *But the anointing which ye have received of him abideth in you.* In both passages the personal pronoun ("ye") is emphatic, accentuating the contrast between John's readers and the antichrists. Weymouth expresses this in verse 20 by translating, "As for you, you have. . . ." ASV uses similar language for verse 27: "And as for you. . . ." Both verses teach, therefore, that this anointing is the peculiar privilege of Christians.

In KJV "unction" (verse 20) and "anointing" (verse 27) translate one Greek word (*chrisma*). It is found in the New Testament only here, but the word is cognate with two other terms used more frequently: *chrio,* "to anoint," used five times; *christos,* "anointed," "Christ," used 569 times.

In the three occurrences of the word in our text (once in verse 20, twice in verse 27) it should be translated uniformly. ASV renders it "anointing"; TCNT, "consecration." NEB sees in it the idea of "initiation." "Anointing" is the most generally accepted definition.

The term signifies not the act of anointing but the element with which the act is performed — literally, "anointing oil," "unguent." Here, however, it is used metaphorically of the Holy Spirit. That is to say, the "anointing" is the Holy Spirit received by the believer in conversion. TEV expresses this: "But you have had the Holy Spirit poured out on you" (verse 20).

The term seems not to have been in common use among Christians, but there are indications that it was current in heretical circles. The gnostics, for example, claimed that they received a special anointing when they were initiated into the secrets of their cult. This anointing, they insisted, gave them an enlightenment and an insight which ordinary believers did not possess.

John appears to be deliberately "borrowing" their term to make his point. In effect, he says to his readers, "Your opponents profess to have an anointing, but it is in their case a false claim. You, on the other hand, have a true anointing. It consists in the gift of the Spirit, it comes from the Holy One (Christ), and it gives a capacity for distinguishing truth from falsehood."

In verse 27 this anointing is said to "abide in" believers. By this John means that their experience of the Holy Spirit is not a temporary thing. He stays with them, remains in them, is retained in their hearts. The statement is intended to give assurance to the readers.

The Christian's anointing gives a capacity for understanding spiritual things. This is mentioned in verses 20 and 21 and in verse 27. "And ye have an anointing from the Holy One, *and ye know all things*" (verse 20, ASV). This means that Christians, by virtue of their anointing, have a knowledge that is certain and complete. It does not mean, however, that they are omniscient. They "know all things" in the sense that they have all the knowledge that is required for salvation. The truth which they possess does not need to be supplemented by the vagaries of gnostic teaching.

The best Greek texts of verse 20b have a different reading, which may be translated "and ye all know." This conveys the thought that knowledge of truth is not, as the gnostics claimed, the prerogative of a favored few, but of all the people of God. TEV: "and so all of you know the truth."

Verse 21 is an expression of the apostle's confidence in the Asian Christians. He writes his warning not because he feels that they "do not know the truth" (verse 21a), but because they "do know it" (verse 21b, TEV). The idea seems to be that their insight into the truth gives John confidence that they will not only understand and appreciate his words but will make proper use of them.

Moreover, John is confident that his readers know *that no lie is of the truth* (verse 21c). That is to say, they recognize the essential and irreconcilable antagonism between truth and falsehood. The "lie" is the pernicious teaching of the antichrists. To say that it is not "of the truth" is to assert that it is utterly foreign to the Christian revelation. It is therefore fraught with danger for the Christian fellowship.

Verse 27 contains the same general teaching which is expressed in verses 20-21, but the language is different: "But the anointing which ye have received of him abideth in you, *and ye need not that any man teach you*" (verse 27a). This does not mean that human teachers are useless, but only that Christians are not ultimately and completely dependent upon them. Ross appropriately comments: "There are many human teachers to whom we shall be for ever grateful but we should not be slavishly dependent on any one of them" (p. 175). Conner explains that the anointing (the Holy Spirit) gives one insight into truth and that this is something which not all the teaching in the world can impart.

The immediate and direct reference may be to the fact that John's readers were in no way dependent upon the gnostic teachers. The reason for this is stated in verse 27b: "For the Spirit [the anointing] teaches you about everything, and what he teaches is true, not false" (TEV).

2. *Their adherence to the Christian message* (verses 24-25). The Greek of verse 24 begins with an emphatic personal pronoun (cf. verses 20, 27) and thus sets John's readers over against the heretics. ASV attempts to express it: *"As for you,* let that abide in you which ye heard from the beginning." It may be paraphrased, "Whatever others may do, you, on your part, let the message which you have known from the beginning of your Christian experience have a permanent place in your hearts." Phillips puts it, "For yourselves I beg you to stick to the original teaching."

In a general sense "that . . . which ye heard from the beginning" is the gospel message. Specifically, in this context, the reference may be to the truth concerning the Father and the Son.

"Let that abide in you . . ." may mean to let the Christian message "be always in your thoughts" (TCNT) or "continue to live in your hearts" (Williams). If you do this, John assures his readers, *ye also shall abide in the Son, and in the Father* (verse 24b, ASV). The pronoun is again emphatic — "you yourselves." "Shall abide," a progressive future, means "shall continue to live." "In the Son, and in the Father" expresses the thought of union with the Son and with the Father.

Mention of this continuous life in union with the Son and with the Father leads John to exclaim, "And this is what he promised us — everlasting life!" (verse 25, Beck). The suggestion is that "everlasting life" is just another name for abiding in the Son and in the Father. It is not simply duration of being which starts at death but a quality of life begun on earth and extending through eternity. Because it is indeed the very life of God it is necessarily indestructible.

3. *Their union with Christ* (verses 27b-28). The key expression in this passage is the phrase *abide in him,* found at the close of verse 27 and at the beginning of verse 28. In the former verse KJV text uses the future tense of the verb ("shall abide"), but undoubtedly the true text has the present tense. In form the Greek word may be either a present indicative (ASV, Weymouth) or a present imperative (NEB, TEV, TCNT, Williams, *et al.*). There is general agreement that in verse 28 it is an imperative.

The word was a favorite with John, being used by him more often than by all the other New Testament writers combined. It occurs twenty-three times in I John (seven times in 2:18-28) and in KJV is translated "continue," "remain," "dwell," and (most often) "abide." "Abiding" in Christ includes both union and communion with Him. The word assumes that we are in Christ, what it commands is that we shall cling tenaciously to Him and draw our strength from Him. In the verse under consideration it means something like "continue to live in union with Him (Christ)." In 3:24 this is associated with keeping Christ's commands.

That, when he shall appear, we may have confidence, and not be ashamed before him at his coming (verse 28b) expresses the purpose or incentive for abiding in Christ.

"When he shall appear" and "at his coming" are references to Christ's return. The word for "appear," used earlier of the unfolding of the whole incarnate life of Christ (1:2) and of the uncovering of the antichrists (2:19), suggests a revealing, an unveiling, a manifestation. The term implies that Christ now lives in glory with the Father and that He and His glory are hidden from the world. At His coming what is now hidden will be revealed.

The word for "coming," found only here in the Johannine writings, occurs rather frequently in the Pauline epistles as a term for the Second Coming of Christ. In the papyri it was a technical term for a royal visit. As applied to the return of Christ it denotes both His arrival and His consequent presence with His people.

"Confidence" translates a word whose primary meaning is "freedom of speech," "unreservedness of utterance." It was the appropriate word to use of the entire freedom with which intimate friends unburdened their hearts to one another. At least one ancient writer used it of the attitude of children to their father in contrast with the attitude of a slave to his master. Used by John nine times in his gospel and four times in this epistle (here, 3:21; 4:17; and 5:14), it connotes, in this context, unreserved confidence, boldness, and courage. It vividly depicts the joyous abandon and the glad fearlessness of those who have an assured conscience.

The opposite of this confidence is to be ashamed. (Compare the "speechlessness" of the wedding guest, Matt. 22:1.) "And not be ashamed before him" may be more literally rendered "and not be shamed away from him." The thought is that of shrinking away from Christ's presence with a feeling of guilt and disgrace.

Griffith Thomas points out that "it is not a question of salvation, but of sorrow at unfaithfulness; it does not mean that we are afraid, but it certainly does indicate the possibility of our feeling utterly ashamed of ourselves, because we have not been true to his wonderful love and grace since our conversion" (p. 278).

FOR FURTHER STUDY

1. Read articles on "Christ," "Antichrist," and "Anointing" in a Bible dictionary.

2. Using a translation other than KJV, make note of every occurrence in I John of the word "abide." Read John 14-16 and mark the occurrences of the same word.

CHAPTER FIVE

The Children of God

(1 John 2:29—3:24)

The commentaries are in general agreement that there is a decided break in thought at the close of chapter 2. (Some make the division at 2:28; some, at 2:29; others, at 3:1.) The concept of fellowship, which has permeated much of the discussion up to this point, now gives place to the thought of the believer's filial relation to God. Expressions such as "begotten of God" and "children of God," which now come into prominence, reflect this shift in emphasis. The Greek word for "beget" occurs ten times from 2:29 to the end of the book, but not at all in 1:1 to 2:28. "Children [sons] of God," which also is absent in the earlier part of the book, is found three times in chapter 3 (verses 1, 2, 10) and once in chapter 5 (verse 2).

The word which John employs for "children" is *tekna*. He never uses for Christians the word *huios* (son), a term frequently found in the writings of Paul. The latter word denotes dignity, status, position, or legal relationship. John's word stresses birth, origin, oneness of nature. Literally it might be rendered "born ones." Paul's word is more in keeping with the idea of adoption. John's term is more in keeping with the idea of regeneration. Both words express important truth about the believer's relation to God.

We will develop our discussion of this section around three matters which pertain to the children of God: (1) their divine origin 2:29); (2) their unique privileges (3:1-3), and (3) their distinguishing marks (3:4-24).

I. THEIR DIVINE ORIGIN (2:29)

Verse 29 is transitional. As such it forms the conclusion of the preceding section and introduces the chief topic of the discussion that follows. Two vital truths are asserted: First, it is God who imparts spiritual life to His people. They are *begotten of him* (ASV). The terminology implies that the Christian has nothing to do with this impartation of life. He neither effects it nor does he actively cooperate in it; he simply receives it.

Interpreters differ as to the reference in "him." In context it is simpler to understand it to mean Christ. This is a problem for some who feel the Scriptures consistently speak of the Father as the agent in our new birth. But compare I Corinthians 4:15 and John 3:5. It is not especially important whether we refer the word to Christ or to the Father, for obviously the point of the statement is that begetting is a divine work.

Second, the practice of righteousness is the evidence of this birth from God. "If ye know that he [Christ] is righteous, *ye know that every one also that doeth righteousness is begotten of him*" (ASV). As it stands, the verse seems to mean that every man who does right is a Christian. In light of this N. Alexander raises a question: "What is John's point? Is he really making unconscious Christians out of, say, conscientious, right-doing humanists? A most un-Johannine idea! John surely has in mind only professing Christians, and means: 'You may be sure that every professing Christian who does right is a Christian in deed and truth' " (p. 76).

It is Christ's nature to *be* righteous. It must be the nature of His people to *do* righteousness. "Doeth" translates a present tense in Greek, indicating that the doing of righteousness is habitual, that it is the ruling principle of one's life. This concept is developed more fully in 3:4-10.

John uses two different words for the idea of knowing. In the first half of the verse "know" (*oida*) speaks of knowledge that is intuitive and absolute. In the second half of the verse "know" (*ginosko*) connotes knowledge gained by experience and observation. The idea then is that we know intuitively, as a matter of principle, that Christ is righteous. We are to "take note" of the fact that everyone who has been begotten of Him practices righteousness. The TCNT renders it, "*Knowing* him to be righteous, you *realize* that every one who lives righteously has received the new Life from him" (italics mine).

Whether "know" is indicative or imperative is debatable. Both Westcott and Law, among others, prefer the latter. Weymouth brings it out in translation: "Since you know that He is righteous, be assured that every one also who acts righteously is a child of His" (cf. NEB, Phillips).

II. THEIR UNIQUE PRIVILEGES (3:1-3)

Having stated that Christians are begotten of God (2:29), the apostle now enlarges on the wonder and glory of their new relationship to God. He mentions (1) their experience of the love of God (verse 1a), (2) their admission to the family of God (verse 1b), and (3) their future sharing in the glory of God (verses 2-3).

1. *Recipients of the love of God* (verse 1a). Although John could look back on a long life filled with the most amazing experiences, he still found the love of God to be an utterly astonishing thing: *Behold, what manner of love the Father hath bestowed upon us.* Conditioned by the Christian message, we are inclined to take the love of God for granted. The ancient world, however, found the wrath of God much easier to grasp than His love.

A sense of adoring wonder is expressed in the phrase "what manner of." A single word in Greek, it always connotes surprise mingled with wonder and astonishment. A good illustration of this is Matthew 8:27: "What manner of man is this, that even the winds and the sea obey him!" (See also Mark 13:1; Luke 1:29; 7:39; II Pet. 3:11, the only other New Testament passages in which the word occurs.) Originally it meant "of what country," but it came to mean "of what sort." Arndt and Gingrich point out that in some contexts the term should be translated "how great" or "how wonderful." Here they prefer "how glorious." Phillips uses the word "incredible." Blaiklock attempts to convey something of the original flavor of the word by rendering the whole phrase "what unearthly love." The suggestion is that God's love is unlike anything else in this world.

2. *Members of the divine family* (verse 1b). The proof of this amazing love-bounty is expressed in verse 1b: *that we should be called children of God* (ASV). The commentaries are not agreed in their understanding of the word "that." Some see it as introducing a purpose clause. God bestowed His love "in order that" we should be called His children. Others take "that" to be declarative, its clause defining that in which the love of God consists. Brooke, who subscribes to this latter view, says the import of the whole statement is to point up the greatness of the divine love.

"Children," as pointed out above, is the translation of a Greek word which literally means "born ones." It follows naturally the assertion in 2:29 of our being born of God. Moffatt attempts to bring this out by repeating the last phrase of verse 29: ". . . is born of him. 'Born of him!' Think what a love the Father. . . ."

"Called" means called by the name of, bear the name of, children of God. It renders a word which was sometimes used in reference to titles of honor. John had in mind the honor which God has bestowed upon us in permitting us to be known as, be named as, His own children.

And we are (Berkeley) shows that we are not only called children of God; we really are His children. These words are not found in KJV, but they are in the best Greek text; all modern translations include them. Spurgeon calls them "a genuine fragment of inspired Scripture . . . too precious to be lost." (See his sermon on these words entitled " 'And We Are': A Jewel from the Revised Version.")

The first readers of this epistle might have thought, "If we are the children of God, why doesn't the world recognize us as such?" John, anticipating their thoughts, adds, *For this cause the world knoweth us not, because it knew him not* (ASV). Moffatt brings out the meaning by rendering the first part of the statement as a question: "The world does not recognize us? That is simply because it did not recognize him." The point is that if the world did not recognize God's Son when He was incarnate, we should not be surprised that it does not recognize us. John's statement implies that the world's hostility to believers is rooted in its rejection of their Lord.

In reading this we should bear in mind what John has previously said about the world and its antagonism to God (2:15-17). Apropos also are the words of Jesus: "If the world hate you, ye know that it hated me before it hated you" (John 15:18).

3. *Partakers of the divine glory* (verses 2-3). Having mentioned the believer's experience of God's love and his admittance into the family of God, John now turns to consider what awaits God's children in the future: *Beloved, now are we children of God, and it is not yet made manifest what we shall be* (verse 2a, ASV). In this sentence the two emphatic expressions are "now" and "not yet." The privileges and dignity of sonship are already ours, but the full disclosure of the glory of our sonship is yet to be. The apostle's words suggest that the Christian's present status is unbelievably wonderful but that his future destiny is even more so.

The tense of "made manifest" suggests that "what we shall be" was never, on any occasion, manifested. In this context the word seems to mean "fully disclosed." Faint inklings of our glorious destiny may be found here and there (e.g., John 14:1 ff; 17:24 ff), but the full manifestation of what is in store for God's children will not come until our Lord returns. (Some interpreters think John means that the believer's destiny has not been manifested to *the world*. Christians, they argue, already know "what we shall be." There seems to be little in the passage to support this view.) For previous uses of the word "manifest" see 1:2; 2:19, 28.

What we do *know* (the word means to know intuitively, unquestioningly, as a matter of principle) is *that, when he* (Christ) *shall appear* (be manifested), *we shall be like him; for we shall see him as he is* (verse 2b). W. Alexander records an incident from the mission field which is a fitting commentary on these words. Some native converts were translating I John. When they came upon the statement, "we shall be like him," the scribe laid down his pen and exclaimed, "No! it is too much; let us write, 'We shall kiss His feet.'" But, as Barrett comments in relating this, "it is not 'too much' for the love of God" (p. 122).

Verse 3 teaches that the anticipation of future conformity to the likeness of Christ is a powerful incentive to growing conformity to that likeness now. *And every one that hath this hope set on him* (Christ) *purifieth himself, even as he* (Christ) *is pure* (ASV). Observe "every one"; there are no exceptions to the principle here stated. (The Greek construction translated "every one" [*pas ho*] is used seven times in the paragraph from 2:29—3:10.)

"Hope" means confident expectation. Its reference here is to our seeing Christ and our being like Him. In writing that our hope is "set on him," John means that our hope of future glory centers in, is fixed upon, the return of Jesus Christ.

The word translated "purifieth" denotes the putting away of all that defiles us. The Septuagint uses it of the high priest's self-purification before entering the Holy of holies. In the New Testament also it is sometimes used of ceremonial cleansing (as in John 11:55), but here it has reference to moral and spiritual cleansing (cf. Jas. 5:8 and I Pet. 1:22). The use of the present tense emphasizes action that is habitual. Some translators see in it the idea of effort. The TCNT, for instance, reads: "And every one who has this hope with regard to Christ tries to make himself pure" (cf. Williams). Ross appropriately observes that though it is only the blood of Christ that can cleanse (1:7), "on each of us rests the responsibility of seeking that cleansing with all our heart" (pp. 180-81).

Believers purify themselves "even as he is pure." This means that Christ, who is eternally pure, is the pattern of our purity, the standard of our conduct. (Compare verse 7, "even as he is righteous.")

III. THEIR DISTINGUISHING MARKS (3:4-24)

One of the recurring emphases of I John is its insistence that one's behavior is an index to his relationship with God. This was stated repeatedly in chapter 2 (verses 3, 4, 6, 9, 15, 29); it is also the thought which dominates the present passage. The two distinguishing traits of the children of God are said to be righteousness and love. The former is developed in verses 4-10; the latter, in 11-24.

1. *Righteousness* (verses 4-10). This was mentioned earlier (2:29) as a characteristic of the begotten of God, but contemplation of the wonder of the new birth and of the love that makes it possible led the apostle to digress momentarily (3:1-3) from his treatment of the theme. Verse 3, with its reference to Christian purity, brings the topic back to mind, and it is enlarged upon in verses 4-10.

The practice of righteousness, discussed previously in 2:3-6, is here enforced by these considerations: (1) the nature of sin (verse 4), (2) the nature of Christ's work (verses 5-8), and (3) the nature of Christian experience (verse 9). The tenth verse forms a concluding summary.

(1) *The nature of sin* (verse 4). Whosoever committeth sin transgresseth also the law: for sin is the transgression of the law. The rendering in KJV is misleading at two important points: First, by using the expression "committeth sin" it obscures the force of the present tense verb; the Greek suggests the doing of sin as a practice, not the committing of an act of sin. Second, by employing the idea of "transgression of the law" KJV mistranslates a Greek word (used in both parts of the verse) which means "lawlessness." "Transgression of the law" (KJV) suggests an act: "lawlessness" denotes the spirit which prompts the act. The ASV correctly reads: "Every one that doeth sin doeth also lawlessness; and sin is lawlessness."

The focal words in John's statement are "sin" and "lawlessness," and they are here equated. The root meaning of the Greek word for sin is failure, "missing the mark." "Lawlessness" suggests rebellion, a flagrant defiance of God. John teaches that all sin — every sin — has this character. The practice of sin, therefore, is totally incompatible with birth from God.

(2) *The purpose of Christ's life and work* (verses 5-8). These verses show that sin is contrary to the whole purpose of our Lord's incarnate ministry. This purpose is expressed in two different ways. The first statement of it is in verse 5: *And ye know that he was manifested to take away our sins: and in him is no sin.* (The second statement, to be treated later, is in verse 8.) "Manifested" (cf. 1:2; 2:19, 28; 3:2 for the same word) refers to Christ's appearing in flesh and includes all that He did in that state. The word implies, though it does not state, the pre-existence of Christ (cf. 1:1, 2).

"Take away" means to lift, to carry, and may here have the notion of taking away by bearing. The term is used in John 1:29 in a similar statment: "Behold, the lamb of God, that taketh away the sin of the world" (ASV).

Observe that the latter passage uses "sin" (singular). The passage which we are considering uses the plural ("sins"). One is the root; the other, the fruit. This gives some support to the view that John the Baptist's statement refers to the expiation of sin (the removal of its guilt) whereas the apostle's statement refers to the believer's sanctification (i.e., causing him to cease from sins). Actually both ideas are implied in each statement.

The sinlessness of Jesus ("and in him is no sin") is that which gives efficacy to His redemptive work.

In verse 6 the apostle draws two conclusions from the preceding statement about Christ's atoning work and sinless life. First,

Whosoever abideth in him sinneth not (verse 6a). This does not mean that a Christian will never commit an act of sin (cf. 1:8— 2:2); it does mean that the Christian does not persist in sin (note the present tense), that sin cannot be the ruling principle in his life. More will be said about this in the discussion of verse 9. Here it should be observed that John states this principle in such sweeping language ("whosoever") that he leaves room for no exceptions.

Second, *whosoever sinneth hath not seen him* (Christ), *neither known him* (verse 6b). This means that the living of a life of sin (present tense) is evidence that one has never (either in the past or now — perfect tense) had vital contact with Christ. He has not "seen" Him with the eye of faith; he has not "known" Him in personal experience. To see and know the sinless Christ breaks the power of sin and makes the life of sin thereafter a moral impossibility.

Verses 7 and 8a contain a solemn warning against being led astray by any one who denies the importance of a righteous life. John teaches that one cannot *be* righteous without *practicing* righteousness. The practice of righteousness shows that one has a moral affinity with Christ (verse 7), and the practice of sin reveals that one is of the devil (verse 8a). *Little children, let no man deceive you: he that doeth righteousness is righteous, even as he* (Christ) *is righteous* (verse 7).

The emphasis is on "doeth," a present tense verb which suggests habitual practice. The thought is that the truly righteous man (a Christian) is a person in whom righteousness is the ruling principle of life. Moreover, the truly righteous man is one for whom Christ is the ultimate standard and pattern of life: "He that doeth righteousness is righteous, *even as he is righteous.*"

Verse 8a states the opposite truth: *He that doeth sin is of the devil* (ASV). "Doeth sin" (cf. "doeth righteousness," verse 7) describes the person who, in a sense, "makes a business of sin." Sin is the persistent habit of his life.

Such a person, John teaches, is "of the devil." That is, he has the devil as his spiritual father (cf. John 8:44) and draws from the devil "the ruling principles of his life" (Westcott, p. 106).

There is, to be sure, a sense in which God is Father of all. That is to say, in the sense that He is the Creator of all, God is the Father of all. But the emphasis of John and of the New Testament generally is upon God's spiritual fatherhood. Only those who are believers in Jesus Christ are truly the children of God. All others, John would say, are the children of the devil.

The practice of sin shows that one has a moral affinity with the devil, for sin is his characteristic activity: *the devil sinneth from the beginning*. The thought appears to be this: Just as the practice of righteousness is the proof that one is born of a God who is righteous (cf. 2:29), so the practice of sin is proof that one's spiritual parentage is in a being who is evil.

"From the beginning" are the emphatic words of this statement. Law takes the meaning to be that the devil is "the aboriginal sinner." Others try to define "the beginning" more specifically: "from the first moment of his being" (Barrett, p. 129), "from the beginning of his diabolical career" (Smith, p. 185), "from the beginning of the human history" (Ramsay, p. 288).

The tense of the verb is present, suggesting that the devil's whole existence is sin. He was the first to sin and he has never ceased to sin.

In verse 5 John stated one purpose of Christ's manifestation, namely, "to take away sins." In verse 8b he gives another: *For this purpose the Son of God was manifested, that he might destroy the works of the devil.* Both statements are intended to show that a life of sin is utterly incongruous in a Christian.

"The works of the devil" are the sins which men commit (cf. "sins," verse 5). Paul calls them "works of darkness" (Rom. 13:12; Eph. 5:11). To "destroy" these is to demolish them, to undo them, put an end to them. The Greek word, which means to loose, to dissolve, to break, and so on, is used in numerous senses in the New Testament—for example, of breaking the law of Moses (John 7:23), of the breaking up of a ship (Acts 27:41), of the dissolving of the marriage tie (I Cor. 7:27), and of the destruction of a dividing wall (Eph. 2:14). In the present passage the word may suggest that the works of the devil (our sins) were like chains binding us. Christ came that He might shatter those chains and loose us from them.

(3) *The nature of Christian experience* (verse 9). The nature of sin (verse 4) and the nature of Christ's work (verses 5-8) are both strong arguments for the believer's antagonism to evil. Verse 9 teaches that what happens to believers in conversion makes the practice of sin an impossibility. The matter is stated in a startling manner: *Whosoever is begotten of God doeth no sin, because his* (God's) *seed abideth in him* (verse 9a, ASV). Moreover, *he cannot sin, because he is begotten of God* (verse 9b, ASV).

The problem raised by this verse is that of reconciling its teaching with what is taught elsewhere in the epistle about the Christian and sin (1:8—2:2). The latter passage teaches that sin is present in every human life; and this teaching, it may be added, is abundantly confirmed in the experience of each of us. On the surface at least, the present passage seems to be stating just the opposite.

To get around this seeming discrepancy, many varying interpretations of verse 9 have been proposed. The following are examples: (1) Some have sought to resolve the difficulty by distinguishing between the soul and the body. They argue that the soul remains pure and unblemished though the body may engage in sin. (It is strange that anyone should propose this, for it is precisely what John's gnostic opponents taught.) (2) Others seek to harmonize this verse with the teaching of 1:8—2:2 by distinguishing between the old nature and the new. They contend that the old nature commits sin but the new nature does no sin. (3) Others circumvent the problem by restricting the meaning of sin to notorious crimes, to flagrant offenses, or to willful and deliberate sin. The Christian, they argue, may commit lesser sins, but he does not commit the more gross sins. (4) Others have explained the verse by saying that John is describing ideal, not actual, Christian experience.. (5) Still others contend that the key which unlocks the problem is found in the meaning of the Greek tenses. In 2:1 "if any man sin" translates a tense (aorist) which suggests occasional lapses into sin. In the verse under consideration "doeth" no sin and "cannot sin" are both present tenses, denoting action that is habitual and persistent. The thought is that one who is begotten of God does not, indeed, cannot, practice sin as a way of life. He may succumb to sin on occasion, but sin is not the habit of his life. Verse 6 is to be interpreted in the same manner.

The child of God does not practice sin "because his [God's] seed abideth in him." Various interpretations of the word "seed" have been given. Moffatt takes it as a collective term for Christians (cf. Isa. 53:10) and understands the word "him" to refer to God: "for the offspring of God remain in Him." The meaning then is that believers do not practice sin because they abide in God.

Augustine, Luther, Alford, Dodd, and others interpret "seed" as a reference to God's Word (cf. Matt. 13:23; John 5:38; I Pet. 1:23; Jas. 1:21). Calvin seems to identify the "seed" with the indwelling Holy Spirit.

We prefer to follow those who interpret the divine "seed" in terms of nature or life-principle. The meaning then is that the child of God does not habitually sin because he has abiding in him a divine life-principle or the divine nature. See RSV ("God's nature abides in him"), TCNT ("the very nature of God dwells within him"), and

Williams ("the God-given life-principle continues to live in him").

(4) *Concluding summary* (verse 10). Throughout this section (beginning at verse 4) John has contrasted the children of God and the children of the devil. Verse 10 sums up the entire discussion: *In this the children of God are manifest, and the children of the devil: whosoever doeth not righteousness is not of God, neither he that loveth not his brother.* "In this" points forward to what is stated in the last half of the verse. "Are manifest" here means something like "plainly distinguished."

John divides the entire race into two classes: "the children of God" and "the children of the devil." As Westcott remarks, "he admits no intermediate class. For him there is only light and darkness, and no twilight. He sees only 'life' and 'death' " (p. 108).

"Doeth" and "loveth," both in the present tense, denote habitual actions.

The manner in which the apostle combines righteousness and love is worthy of notice. The suggestion is that where one is the other will also be found. That is to say, a life of righteousness is a life of love. Indeed, love may be thought of as the highest expression of righteousness.

The mention of "righteousness" points back to 2:29. With the reference to love John glides into the leading topic of the following verses.

2. *Love* (verses 11-24). Righteousness has been presented as an evidence of divine sonship (3:4-10). Now the apostle discusses love as a second evidence of that relationship (cf. 2:7-17).

Verses 11 and 12 are transitional. Combining the ideas of love and righteousness, they might be construed either with that which precedes them or with the verses which follow. We prefer the latter construction.

There are four leading statements under which the teaching of this passage may be summarized:

(1) *Love is the burden of the apostolic message* (verses 11-12). This was suggested in 2:7 and 8 by John's reference to love as "an old commandment which ye had from the beginning." But the concept is stated much more emphatically here: *For this is the message which ye heard from the beginning, that we should love one another* (verse 11).

The word "message" is used here, as in 1:5, to sum up a truth of profound importance. In 1:5 the term is employed to set forth a fundamental teaching concerning the character of God ("God is light"). Here it is used to point up a fundamental duty of the Chris-

tian life ("love one another"). The former (1:5) is a summary of
Christian theology; the latter (3:11), a summary of Christian ethics.
Outside of these two verses the Greek word for "message" is not
found in the New Testament.

"From the beginning" should be compared with 2:7, where the
same phrase is used in a similar context. Here, as there, the reference is probably to the beginning of the readers' Christian life.

"That" represents a different Greek word from the "that" of
1:5. There is a hint of purpose ("in order that") here which is not
found in the earlier passage. Findlay may therefore be correct in
saying that 1:5 gives the content of the Christian message; 3:11
states its effect or issues.

Verse 12 shows that hate, the opposite of love, is the mark of
those who are the children of the devil. This is illustrated in Cain,
whom John represents as the prototype of the devil's progeny. Evidence that he was *of the evil one* is found in the fact that he *slew* —
the word means "slaughtered," "butchered" — *his brother*. This he
did, explains John, because *his own works were evil, and his
brother's righteous*. Barrett remarks: "Then, as now, the surest
proof of the wickedness of the child of the devil is this, that he is
stung into fury, not merely by some wrong done to him, but simply
by the spectacle of the goodness of the child of God" (p. 136).

Law thinks that the sinister figure of Cain is introduced at this
point in order to set forth the more clearly, by way of contrast, the
self-sacrificing love of Christ (verse 16). "Cain sacrificed his brother's life to his own wounded self-love; Christ sacrificed His own life
in love to His brethren. . . . And every man belongs to the brotherhood either of Cain or of Christ" (pp. 242-43).

The words "righteous" and "righteousness," so prominent in the
epistle to this point, do not occur again.

(2) *Love is the proof that we have passed out of death into
life* (verses 13-15). Verse 13 is brought in almost as a parenthesis.
Marvel not, brethren, if the world hateth you (ASV). "Marvel not"
means that we are not to be astonished nor surprised at the world's
hostility to the people of God. The statement was probably suggested
by the reference to Cain's motive in the killing of his brother. It
implies that the Cain-spirit is not dead; righteousness still provokes
the hostility of those who belong to Satan.

Verse 14, however, teaches that the real evidence of our new
life is not in the world's hostility but in our love. Whatever the
world may think or say, *We* (emphatic) *know that we have passed
out of death into life, because we love the brethren* (ASV). "Know"

renders the word (*oida*) which means to know intuitively, to know with positive certitude.

"Have passed" translates a Greek verb which was used in ancient times of persons migrating from one country to another country. (Compare John 13:1, where the same word is used of Jesus' departure from this world to the Father.) It is in the perfect tense, suggesting an act accomplished in the past with results continuing in the present. We have passed out of death and into life, and life is now our permanent and abiding state.

The statement about our passing out of death into life is followed by a parallel statement suggesting the opposite: *He that loveth not abideth in death* (ASV). Observe that "loveth" is not limited by an object. ("His brother" in KJV is poorly attested.)

The tense of the verb translated "abideth" is present, suggesting that death is the natural state of such a person. The NEB renders it: "The man who does not love is still in the realm of death."

This idea is enlarged upon in the fifteenth verse: *Whosoever hateth his brother is a murderer: and ye know that no murderer hath eternal life abiding in him.* "Hateth," a present tense, describes a person for whom hatred is a way of life. Such a person, John affirms, is essentially a murderer, even though he may never commit the overt act. The statement is reminiscent of the teaching of Jesus (Matthew 5:21-22).

"Ye know" means you know as a matter of principle, you know intuitively, so that instruction is not needed on this matter.

The steps in John's argument are deeply significant: "not loving" (verse 14) is "hating" (verse 15); "hating" is "murder" (verse 15); and murder reveals that one does not possess the life of God (verse 15b).

(3) *Love has its supreme revelation in the sacrificial death of Christ* (verses 16-18). This is stated in verse 16a: *Hereby know we love, because he laid down his life for us* (ASV). "Hereby" looks forward to the "because" clause. The word translated "know" means to come to know, to become acquainted with, to know by experience. The thought is that we have become aware of love, have learned what it really is. The tense is perfect, indicating that the knowledge gained continues with us. "We have learnt and now hold the lesson for ever" (Westcott, p. 114).

"Love" stands in the text without qualifying words. ("Of God," placed in italics in KJV, should be omitted.) The emphasis therefore is on love in its nature, what it is. John teaches that we could not have known this had not Christ "laid down his life for us." Laying down one's life is the same as giving one's self. The words teach therefore that Christ's death was a voluntary self-sacrifice in behalf of sinners.

Verse 16b draws an inference from the statement about Christ's self-giving love. He laid down His life for us; *We too, then, ought to give our lives for our brothers* (verse 16b, TEV). There is a sense, of course, in which Christ's deed was unique. It had a redemptive, propitiatory significance which can never attach to anything which we do. But as an expression of sacrificial love and service it is the pattern for us to copy (cf. Phil. 2:5 ff.; I Pet. 2:21 ff.).

The "we" (emphatic in Greek) means we as His followers, we on our part. The TEV brings out the emphasis by rendering it "we too."

"Ought," a particularly strong word, means to be indebted, to be bound, to do a thing. Here it speaks of our obligation to reproduce Christ's self-giving love. If the good of our Christian brothers — such is the primary meaning of "brethren" in I John — should require it, we are obligated "to lay down our lives" for them.

Most of us may never find it necessary actually to lay down our lives for others, but self-giving love is a principle to which all of us must be dedicated. Findlay reminds us that in John's day the duty here stated was "no stretch of an heroic fancy. Every Christian held himself at the disposal of the community. At any time martyrdom might be called for; already many a dear life had been laid down for the brethren's sake" (p. 280).

In verse 17 the apostle teaches that in other, less dramatic ways, all of us are to demonstrate the genuineness of our love. It is put in the form of a rhetorical question: *But whoso hath the world's goods, and beholdeth his brother in need, and shutteth up his compassion from him, how doth the love of God* (i.e., love for God) *abide in him?* (ASV). The manner in which the question is raised implies that anyone who sees others in need and refuses to share with them could not possibly have love for God abiding in him (cf. James 2:15-16). The best commentary on these words is John's own statement: "For he that loveth not his brother whom he hath seen, how can he love God whom he hath not seen?" (4:20).

The picture is vividly drawn. The person in question *has* worldly goods (the things needed to sustain life) and sees (gazes on) a Christian brother who *has* (same word as above) need. "The one *has* as his possession *wealth*, the other *has* as his possession — *need*" (Plummer, p. 85).

"Beholdeth" indicates more than a passing glance. It implies consideration, a lingering look (as at a spectacle). "Shutteth up his compassion" denotes the slamming of the heart's door so that the destitute brother is left without access to sympathy and help. This is a far cry from the self-giving love of verse 16.

Findlay writes: "In many a Church the man is found singing with unction,

> 'Were the whole realm of nature mine
> That were a present far too small!'

for whose shrunken soul the smallest coin out of a full purse proves large enough to meet Christ's loudest appeal" (p. 281).

Verse 18 is a warning against making talk a substitute for deeds of compassion: *My little children, let us not love in word, neither with the tongue; but in deed and truth* (ASV). The NEB says, "My children, love must not be a matter of words or talk; it must be genuine, and show itself in action." Ramsay comments that "the love of idle sentiment and the love that ends in soothing words . . . is not the love that led Christ to the Cross" (p. 295).

(4) *Love brings assurance of our standing before God* (verses 19-24). Verses 19 and 20 are generally conceded to be the most difficult verses in the epistle, mainly because of the complexity of the grammar. For instance, opinions vary concerning the punctuation of the verses,[1] the meaning of the word translated "assure" (KJV),[2] the translation of the first two Greek words of verse 20,[3] and the use of the conjunction with which verse 20b begins.[4] The reader should consult several translations to see for himself the numerous ways in which the text may be rendered.

Though the majority of recent translations and commentaries take other approaches, we are following KJV in placing a full stop at the end of verse 19. Moreover, we believe KJV and ASV are correct in reading the first word of verse 20 as a causal conjunction and in preserving the conditional force of the second word of the verse. To fail to do this is to obscure the meaningful parallelism of verses 20

---

[1]Some (e.g., KJV) put a period at the end of verse 19; some (e.g., ASV), a colon; others (e.g., RSV), no punctuation mark at all. (Some commentators put a period at the end of verse 19a and begin a new paragraph with 19b.)

[2]"Persuade" (Rotherham), "convince" (NEB), "reassure" (RSV).

[3]KJV, "for if"; RV, "whereinsoever"; RSV, "wherever"; NEB, "that even if."

[4]Some (KJV, ASV, and NEB, for example) take it to be redundant and leave it untranslated; RSV and others translate it "for" or "because"; Alford and others understand an ellipsis before the conjunction and supply "it is": "because if our heart condemns us, (it is) because . . . ."

and 21 ("For if our heart condemn us [verse 20]. . . . Beloved, if our heart condemn us not" [verse 21]).

Having mentioned the problems relating to the structure and translation of the passage, let us look now at its meaning. All of it, as indicated above, concerns assurance. The fact of assurance is stated in verse 19; an explanation of the importance of assurance is given in verse 20; some deductions are drawn in verses 21-24.

(a) *The possibility of assurance* (verse 19). Verse 19 teaches that the presence of genuine love in our lives makes possible two wonderful experiences: (1) knowing that we are of the truth and (2) assuring our consciences before God. The first of these is stated in verse 19a: *Hereby shall we know that we are of the truth* (ASV). "Hereby" is retrospective, pointing back to the idea of loving in deed and truth (verse 18).

"Shall we know" denotes a knowledge that is experiential. "We shall come to know" or "get to know" or "ascertain" is the idea.

To be "of the truth," which is about the same as to be "of God," denotes a condition of spiritual affinity with the truth of God as it is in Jesus (cf. John 14:6; 18:27). Knox renders it, "we take our character from the truth"; TCNT, "we are on the side of the Truth"; Moffatt, "we belong to the truth."

Second, in the practice of genuine love not only shall we come to know that we are of the truth; in addition, we *shall assure our heart before him* (God) (verse 19b, ASV). The context implies that this assurance is possible only if we know that we are of the truth. That is to say, this statement follows the former one as a logical consequence.

"Shall assure," which is coordinate with "shall know," translates a word which basically means "to persuade." In this context it takes on the meaning of "pacify," "still," "soothe," "reassure" (RSV). The *Confraternity New Testament* beautifully renders it "we set our hearts at rest."

"Heart," in the Bible, often stands for the whole inner man — emotion, intellect, will. Here, however, it seems to be used much as we use the word "conscience."

"Before him" (literally, "in his [God's] presence") is placed at the beginning of the Greek clause for emphasis. The stress of the entire statement, therefore, rests on these words. It is a thing of small consequence for the conscience to be soothed and reassured in and by itself; but if the assuring of conscience is done under the searching eye of God, that is something else.

(b) *The importance of assurance* (verse 20). Verse 20 is

an enlargement upon the idea of assuring our hearts *in God's presence*.[5] That is to say, it explains why such heart assurance is so vitally important. *If our heart condemn us, God is greater than our heart, and knoweth all things* (ASV). These words are directed at the person who has no loving deeds by which to assure his heart before God. He has loved in word and tongue, not in deed and truth, and his conscience convicts him.[6] John's statement reminds such a person that if his own ignorant and partial conscience condemns him, the verdict of an omniscient God will be even more severe.

Findlay adds: "Even when a man's heart absolves him, he may not for this reason presume on God's approval: 'I know nothing against myself,' writes St. Paul, 'yet not on this ground am I justified. But he that trieth me is the Lord' (I Cor. 4:4). How much more must one fear, when conscience holds him guilty!" (p. 303).

That the word "condemn" is in the present tense is not to be overlooked. Suggesting repeated or continuous accusations of conscience, it emphasizes the seriousness of the situation. As Findlay says, it "implies not a passing cloud but a persistent shadow, a repeated or sustained protest of conscience" (p. 302).

(c) *The fruit of assurance* (verses 21-24). Assurance of our standing before God issues in two further benefits: boldness toward God (verse 21) and assurance of effectiveness in prayer (verse 22).

Beloved, if our heart condemn us not, then have we confidence toward God (verse 21). The affectionate address ("Beloved") seems

---

[5] It is a much-debated question whether the import of verse 20 is consolatory or condemnatory; that is, whether the verse was written as a statement of *comfort* and encouragement to the overscrupulous (cf. Bunyan's Mr. Fearing) or as a *warning* to the overconfident. Nearly all recent interpreters prefer the former view. They understand John to mean that if our hearts condemn us we can appeal to God for reassurance. Our hearts, they argue, condemn us on partial knowledge; God, who knows all — our weaknesses, our intentions, our circumstances, His own provision for our sins, etc. — assesses our condition on a more reliable basis. Those who advocate this approach often quote Peter's words: "Lord, thou knowest all things, thou knowest that I love thee" (John 21:17).

Proponents of the other view understand the verse as a warning to those who do not practice genuine love. The thought, according to these interpreters, is that if our hearts condemn us, God will all the more condemn us. Among others, Calvin, Alford, and Findlay take this approach. To the present writer their arguments are somewhat more convincing than the arguments for the other view. The reader will find Findlay's discussion most illuminating.

[6] Alford thinks verse 20 is a general statement about the need for assurance and that there is no specific reference to heart condemnation for lack of loving deeds.

to suggest John's relief in leaving the ominous warning which he felt constrained to give in verse 20. That verse is filled with shadows; this verse opens up a brighter scene.

The word translated "confidence" means here, as in the other places where it is used in this epistle, "frankness of speech," "unreservedness," "boldness." It bespeaks the attitude of one who has nothing to hide. Findlay calls it "the 'freedom' of happy children who have access always to the Father" (p. 305). Stott describes it as "a communion with God which is free and unrestricted" (p. 148).

Whatsoever we ask, we receive of him, because we keep his commandments, and do those things that are pleasing in his sight (verse 22). The ASV begins this verse with "And," suggesting that it is our boldness toward God (verse 21) that gives us this assurance of success in prayer. As Ross says, "Children who come so confidently to their Heavenly Father cannot ask anything that He will refuse" (p. 193).

Observe that the assurance of answered prayer is stated in the most unqualified manner: "whatsoever we ask." The last half of the verse tells how this can be. It is "because we keep his commandments, and do those things that are pleasing in his sight." "Our prayers are answered because our wills are at one with the will of God" (Ramsay, p. 296).

An obedient life is an expression of harmony with God. Therefore, the man whose primary concern is keeping God's commandments and doing the things that please Him is not likely to ask for something which is contrary to the will of God.

Verse 23 defines God's commandments. *And this is his commandment, that we should believe* (aorist tense, a once-for-all event) *in the name of his Son Jesus Christ, and love* (present tense, a continuous practice) *one another, even as he gave us commandment* (ASV). The "name" of Christ is Christ as He is revealed to us in the gospel. Among the Jews one's name summed up his nature, his character. The word, therefore, was almost equivalent to our "person."

To "believe" in the name (the case construction in Greek is somewhat unusual) is to accept as true all that Christ is and has done for us, to give credence to everything that Christ's name stands for. (This is the first time believing has been referred to in the epistle.)

In addition to believing in Christ, we are to "love one another." These two commandments — believe in Christ and love the brethren — are brought together so closely that John can speak of them as a single "commandment." We infer from this that there is no true belief in the name of Christ apart from a love for His people. And there is no true love for His people apart from belief in the name of the Son.

Verse 24 is transitional. The first part rounds out the discussion of love; the last part introduces the discussion of 4:1-6. The reference to keeping God's commandments (verse 24a) points up that obedience is both the condition and the proof that we abide in God and He in us. Apart from such obedience intimate communion with God is impossible.

The mutual abiding, mentioned here for the first time in the epistle, is developed more fully in chapter 4 (verses 13-16). What is stated in the present passage echoes the teaching of Jesus in John 15:1-11.

Verse 24b contains the epistle's first reference to the Holy Spirit by name (cf. 2:20, 27). It teaches that the presence of the Spirit in us confirms the indwelling of God: *And hereby we know that he abideth in us, by the Spirit which he hath given us.* "Hereby" looks forward to "by the Spirit. . . ."

Most commentators feel that the "hereby" of verse 24 answers to the "hereby" of verse 19. That verse, they explain, gives, the outward, practical evidence that we are "of the truth." This verse gives the inward subjective evidence that God dwells in us (cf. Rom. 8: 16). But there may be more here than just the thought of an inward witness borne by the Holy Spirit to our spirit.[7] John may have been thinking of the fact that it is the indwelling Spirit who inspires us to confess Jesus as the incarnate Son of God (4:1-6) and who empowers us to live in righteousness and love (Gal. 5:16, 22). If, therefore, we are to have full assurance, "we must look for evidence of the Spirit's working, and particularly whether He is enabling us to believe in Christ, to obey God's commandments and to love the brethren" (Stott, p. 151).

FOR FURTHER STUDY

1. Read articles on "Son," "Child," "Beget," "New Birth," "Righteousness," and "Love" in a Bible dictionary.

---

[7]Law, noting the connection of 3:24b with 4:1-6, contends that the Spirit is here "regarded simply as the inspirer of the True Confession of Jesus. If we make this confession, it is evidence that the spirit in us is the Spirit of God. Thus 'we know that God abideth in us by the Spirit He hath given us'" (p. 263).

2. Mark the occurrences of the words "beget," "begotten," "born," in I John 2:29—3:24.

3. Using a concordance, look up passages in which the word "boldness" occurs.

4. Spurgeon has seven sermons on texts found in I John 3. Some of the titles: "The Sinful Made Sinless," "Life Proved by Love," "What is the Verdict?" and "The Conditions of Power in Prayer."

CHAPTER SIX

True and False Spirits

(1 John 4:1-6)

In a passage which is of considerable importance for the study of I John 4:1 ff. Paul mentions a divine gift which he designates as the "discerning of spirits" (I Cor. 12:10). This gift consisted in a special insight or a special ability to distinguish between true manifestations of the Spirit and counterfeit (Satanic) manifestations. The apostle had in mind spiritual manifestations in and through human beings who claimed to be prophets (spokesmen for God).

From the context of the Corinthian passage we conclude that not every believer had this gift; those who did possess it, however, were thereby enabled to identify the true prophet and to recognize the divine origin of his message. Persons thus gifted rendered an especially valuable service in a period when the church was surging with life and congregational worship was characterized by exuberant and diverse spiritual activity.

The similar teaching of I Thessalonians 5:20-21 is more like that of the passage before us. In both of these passages *every* Christian is put under obligation to test prophetic utterances purporting to come from God. It is asumed, therefore, that even the humblest believer has the capacity for doing this and that no spiritual endowment is required other than what is common to all Christians (cf. I John 2:20, 27).

In approaching the present passage, at least three things should be kept in mind: First, we should keep in mind the intimate connection which these verses sustain with the closing verse of chapter

3. That verse serves as a kind of text upon which this paragraph is an amplification.

Second, we should remember the controversial setting of this epistle. John was not opposing people who were professed pagans but people who claimed to be Christians, who claimed to possess the Holy Spirit, and who claimed to speak with profound spiritual insight (cf. 2:18-28). "They spoke, as it seemed, with a Christian tongue, but none the less they were deadly opponents of Christianity and of Christ" (Barrett, p. 152).

Third, we must remember that church services in apostolic times were quite different from the placid and powerless meetings all too common in our day. Ours are formal and rigidly predictable. Theirs were extremely informal and unstructured. The whole atmosphere pulsated with spiritual life. Moreover, each church would have several elders, and even visitors were generally free to address the congregation. Unprincipled people could easily take advantage of the situation. John, therefore, cautions his readers against being duped by persons falsely claiming to speak in and for the Spirit of God. (Compare I Cor. 12:1-4; II Cor. 11:4; II Thess. 2:2.)

The passage contains a command (verse 1), an explanation (verses 2-3), and an assurance (verses 4-6).

I. THE COMMAND (verse 1)

Beloved, believe not every spirit, but try the spirits whether they are of God (verse 1a). For the fourth time (cf. 2:7; 3:2, 21) the writer addresses his readers with the affectionate and tender term "beloved." Its use here may suggest the seriousness of the matter about to be treated.

The command itself is twofold: "believe not every spirit" and "try the spirits." Both reflect a church situation charged with spiritual enthusiasm and doctrinal controversy.

A key word throughout this passage is "spirit." Goodspeed interprets it to mean "inspired utterance"; Williams, "spiritual utterance"; TCNT, "inspiration." Lamsa, translating the Syriac text, uses "prophecy." Knox, who renders the Latin, employs "prophetic spirit." Calvin may not be exactly correct in understanding "spirit" as a metonym for prophet, but his approach does no real violence to the text. Following Calvin, one would read "prophet" everywhere the word "spirit" occurs in these six verses.

Calvin's interpretation does, however, obscure the obvious connection of this passage with the reference to the Holy Spirit in 3:24.

Moreover, the use of "spirit" rather than "prophet" shows that the apostle was looking behind and beyond the individual prophet to the superhuman influence which inspired him. Strictly speaking, then, the "spirit" is the spirit possessing the prophet and is not to be explained metonymically.

"Believe not every spirit" means do not give credence to every spirit, do not accept as true every prophetic utterance just because the man who makes it claims to be speaking under divine inspiration. It is possible that his inspiration comes from a source other than God. "True faith examines its object before reposing confidence in it" (Stott, p. 152).

The verb is a present imperative, which with the negative may mean "stop believing" (Williams).

To "try the spirits" is to test them for authenticity. The verb was used in ancient times of the testing of metals for genuineness. In Luke 14:19 it is employed by the man who said, "I have bought five yoke of oxen, and I go to *prove* them." In other places it is used of "proving" the will of God (Rom. 12:2), of the "testing" of every man's work by fire (I Cor. 3:13), of God "trying" the heart (I Thess. 2:4), and so forth. It is the word used by Paul in I Thessalonians 5:21: *"Prove* all things; hold fast that which is good."

Ordinarily the word denoted a testing which carried with it the expectation of approval. It thus suggests, as Blaiklock observes, "a good and hopeful aim, a proving with the desire in mind that the object proved may stand the test. We are not to be eager to impute error, to find fault and heresy where none is intended. We are not to apply tests and canons of our own invention, eager to demonstrate that all the rest are wrong, and we alone are right. Too often has orthodoxy shown that spirit, and antagonized where it might have reconciled, and spoiled all testimony to truth by a lamentable lack of love which belies truth quite as vital" (p. 53).

The purpose of testing the spirits is to determine their origin, that is, *whether they are of God.* Plummer remarks that this verse "shews us in what spirit to judge of such things as the reported miracles at Lourdes and the so-called 'manifestations' of Spiritualism. When they have been proved to be real, they must still further be proved to see 'whether they are of God.' We are not to judge of doctrine by miracles, but of miracles by doctrine. A miracle enforcing what contradicts the teaching of Christ and His Apostles is not 'of God' and is no authority for Christians" (pp. 94-95).

The need for testing the spirits is stated in the last part of the verse: *because many false prophets are gone out into the world*

(1b). "Prophets" were sometimes foretellers of the future, but mainly they were forthtellers of a message. They were "mouthpieces" or spokesmen for God. In this context the "false prophets" were heretical teachers who claimed to be instruments of the Holy Spirit but who were in fact spokesmen and instruments of an evil spirit. They are to be identified with the "many antichrists" of 2:18 ff.

"World" does not here have the sinister connotation which usually attaches to it in this epistle. The context suggests that it means simply the world of men.

II. AN EXPLANATION (verses 2-3)

These verses explain that the test by which true and false spirits are to be distinguished is doctrinal. The crux of it is the rejection or acceptance of Jesus Christ as the incarnate Son of God: *Hereby know ye the Spirit of God: Every spirit that confesseth that Jesus Christ is come in the flesh is of God* (verse 2). The word "hereby" points forward to the words which follow the colon. The word translated "know" means "to apprehend," "to recognize," "to perceive." The NEB: "This is how we may recognize the Spirit of God: every spirit which. . . ." In form the Greek word may be either an imperative or an indicative. Either yields an acceptable sense, but most scholars prefer to read it as an indicative.

"Every spirit that confesses" is a reference to prophetic utterances made under the claim of divine inspiration. Calvin, as explained above, takes "every spirit" to mean "every prophet." (In like manner "Spirit of God," in the foregoing clause, is understood as "prophet of God.") "Confesseth" means, in this context, "to declare openly," "to acknowledge boldly."

The essence of the confession is "that Jesus Christ is come in the flesh." In it there is a great truth implied (the preexistence of Christ) and a great truth asserted (Christ's real Incarnation). Every word is important and will repay careful study. For instance, it should be remembered that in I John "Christ" does not denote simply the Messiah of Old Testament prophecy. In John's vocabulary the term denotes the divine preexistent personality of Jesus and is equivalent to "Son of God."

It is also worthy of notice that the preposition is "in," not "into." Many of the gnostics taught that the divine Christ descended upon the man Jesus at the baptism and thus came "into" flesh at that time. John, on the other hand, says that the Christ came "in" flesh, the idea being that He was essentially one with Jesus. The statement reflects the assertion of John's gospel that "the Word became flesh" (1:14).

"Flesh" speaks here of human nature. "He became a real man, of the same nature with us, that he might become our brother, except that he was free from every sin and corruption" (Calvin, p. 232).

"Is come," which translates a perfect tense, means that the Incarnation is an abiding reality, a permanent, not a temporary, union of God and man. Jesus Christ is God and man, in one Person, forever.

A more literal rendering of the whole phrase is, "every spirit which confesses Jesus Christ (as) having come in flesh." This translation makes "Jesus Christ" the object of the verb and "having come in flesh" the predicate.

Others, changing the emphasis slightly, prefer to read it "every spirit which confesses Jesus (as) the Christ having come in flesh." This translation makes "Jesus" the object of the verb and "Christ having come in flesh" the predicate. Compare Moffatt: "Every spirit which confesses Jesus as the Christ incarnate comes from God."

Both of these translations correctly point up that the confession is the confession of a *Person* (Jesus Christ) in a certain character ("having come in flesh"). The KJV suggests that the confession is the acknowledgment of the truth of a certain proposition about Christ, namely, that He has come in the flesh. This is somewhat misleading, for the confession is "not of the fact of the Incarnation, but of the Incarnate Christ" (Brooke, p. 109).

From this verse we gather that the crucial matter in testing the spirits is to determine the attitude of the prophet toward Jesus Christ. "As Christ is the object at which faith aims," writes Calvin, "so he is the stone at which all heretics stumble" (p. 232). No prophetic utterance is to be received as coming from the Spirit of God if that utterance does not acknowledge Jesus Christ to be the incarnate Son of God.

Before leaving this verse one observation is in order: Much that is said about Jesus in current theological debate is nothing other than the reappearance in modern guise of the old gnostic heresy which John was opposing. The apostle insisted that the eternal divine-human person of Christ is a truth so basic to Christianity that it can never be compromised. "Jesus Christ having come in flesh" is not merely the heart of the Gospel but the whole of it.

Verse 3a, in typical Johannine style, states the opposite of the preceding verse: *And every spirit that confesseth not that Jesus Christ is come in the flesh is not of God.* The RSV translates a better Greek text: "and every spirit which does not confess Jesus is not of God." The Greek has an article before "Jesus," suggesting that the reference is to "the" Jesus set forth in the foregoing verse. Smith renders it "the aforementioned Jesus" (p. 189). The NEB: "and every spirit which does not thus acknowledge Jesus is not from God."

The latter part of verse 3 identifies the false prophets (verse 1) and their doctrine (verse 3a) with the "antichrist." *And this is the spirit of the antichrist, whereof ye have heard that it cometh; and now it is in the world already* (ASV). The meaning is that the heretical teaching being refuted here is an expression of the spirit of antichrist already condemned in chapter 2. "This" refers to the denial of Jesus (verse 3a).

In "the spirit of the antichrist" the word "spirit" is italicized to indicate that there is no equivalent word in the Greek text. Perhaps we should understand something like "characteristic": "and this (the denial of Jesus) is the distinguishing characteristic of the antichrist." Law paraphrases it: "And this that we have been speaking of — all these undivine manifestations — are [sic] the fulfillment of the current expectation of Antichrist" (p. 396).

III. AN ASSURANCE (verses 4-6)

Verses 4, 5, and 6 each begin with an emphatic personal pronoun: "Ye" (verse 4), "They" (verse 5), and "We" (verse 6). The words refer respectively to John's readers (i.e., true Christians), the false prophets, and John (as representative of those who proclaimed the apostolic message). The burden of each verse is to give the readers assurance and encouragement in their struggle with error.

1. *The victory of John's readers* (verse 4). The aim of verse 4 was to hearten the readers so that "they might courageously and boldly resist impostors" (Calvin, p. 234). The apostle accomplishes this, first, by assuring them of their divine origin. *Ye are of God, little children.* That is to say, you, rather than the false prophets, derive your spiritual life from God and are His true people. "Therefore," John seems to say, "don't be afraid of those who oppose you."

John further encourages his readers by reminding them of their victory in the conflict with error: *Ye . . . have overcome them* (cf. 2:14). The "overcoming" perhaps refers both to a personal victory and a church victory. Personally, John's readers had resisted the seductive teaching of their opponents and had refused to be taken in by their deceptions. As a congregation, they had refuted their arguments and had been successful in keeping them from corrupting the church.

Everything in this epistle implies that though the initial battle had been won by those who were "valiant for truth," the conquest over error was not complete. Yet the verb ("have overcome") is a perfect tense, suggesting that the victory has been won and its results abide. Alford remarks that "there need not be any evading or softening of this perfect. . . . It is faith outrunning sight: the victory is certain" (p. 1737). The NEB conveys the sense: "you have the mastery."

The reason for their victory is stated in the last part of verse 4: *because greater is he that is in you, than he that is in the world.* The language suggests that the victory, in the truest sense, was God's. Calvin comments: "We can no more be conquered than God himself, who has armed us with his own power to the end of the world" (p. 234).

"He that is in you" is the Spirit of God (cf. 3:24). "He that is in the world" is Satan. (Note that "the world" is practically identified with the false prophets. The next verse brings out the close relationship existing between them.)

The entire verse is an echo of the words spoken by Christ on the night of His arrest: "Be of good cheer; I have overcome the world" (John 16:33).

2. *The worldly character of the false prophets* (verse 5). "It is no small consolation," writes Calvin, "that they who dare to assail God in us, have only the world to aid and help them" (p. 235). *They* (in contrast with "Ye," verse 4) *are of the world.* That is to say, they (the false prophets) come from the world, they derive their "commission" from it. Therefore, they are its delegates, its "apostles," its "prophets." The "world" is the realm of evil (5:19), of hostility to God (2:15-17).

Because the false prophets are of the world, *they speak* — the Greek word may have the sense of "prating" — *of the world.* This means that they derive both their inspiration and their message from the world. It should therefore come as no surprise that the world hears them (cf. John 15:19). As D. Smith observes, "The world listens to those who speak its own language" (p. 190). And Calvin remarks that "it is nothing new or unusual that the world, which is wholly fallacious, should readily hearken to what is false" (p. 235).

An observation: We do well to remember that a man is not necessarily preaching truth just because his ministry attracts large crowds. "Eliminate the obligation of righteousness, the necessity of the spirit of love, and faith in the Divine personality of Jesus Christ," writes Ramsay, "and there remains a teaching which 'the world' applauds, in which it finds an echo of its own sentiments" (pages 301-02).

3. *The divine inspiration of apostolic preachers* (verse 6). *We* (as opposed to the false prophets, verse 5) *are of God*. The "we" may perhaps be an editorial plural referring only to John. It is more probable, however, that John uses the plural to include with himself all those who preached the apostolic message.

"Of God" is in contrast to "of the world" (verse 5). So for a Christian teacher to be "of God" is for him to derive his commission, his message, and his inspiration from God.

This being so, John can write: *he that knoweth God heareth us; he that is not of God heareth not us.* False prophets are of the world, speak the language of the world, and the world listens to them. John and others like him, being of God speak the language of God, and those who know God listen to them; worldly people, who have no affinity with the apostolic message, do not listen to them.

These daring words reflect John's profound sense of authority and certitude. They would obviously be out of place on the lips of one who was not conscious of apostolic authority. As Stott says, "No private believer could presume to say: 'whoever knows God agrees with me; only those who are not of God disagree with me'" (p. 158).

However, there is a principle implied here which is worthy of notice, namely, that God's Word elicits a positive response from God's people because there is a deep and real affinity between the two. Jesus alluded to this when He declared that His sheep know and hear His voice (John 10:4, 5, 8, 16, 27), that everyone who is of the truth hears His voice (John 10:27), and that he who is of God hears the words of God (John 8:47). It is this very point that John makes when he asserts that since "we [the apostolic preachers] are of God" everyone who knows God "listens to us" (the apostolic preachers). Those who refuse to listen and submit to the apostolic message pass judgment on themselves.

The last statement of verse 6 summarizes the foregoing discussion: *Hereby know we the spirit of truth, and the spirit of error.* "Hereby" (cf. 2:3, 5; 3:16, 19, 24; 4:2) points back to the two tests which have been proposed: (1) the content of the message proclaimed (verses 2-3), and (2) the character of the audience attracted (verses 5-6).[1] "Know" means here "to distinguish," "to recognize."

Most commentaries take "the spirit of truth" to be the Holy Spirit (cf. John 14:17; 15:26; 16:13) and "the spirit of error" to be Satan. Alford, for example, explains that "both the Spirit of Truth and the spirit of error speak by the spirits of men who are their organs" (p. 1736). And Law writes that "the 'spirits' on either side are many, yet have one head and represent one character — the Spirit of Truth and the Spirit of Error (4:6)" (p. 264).

The gist of the whole statement is that those who acknowledge Jesus as the incarnate Son of God thereby give evidence that they speak for the Holy Spirit and by His power. On the other hand, those who do not make this confession of Christ give evidence that they are controlled and inspired by Satan.[2]

For Further Study

1. Read articles on "Spirit," "Truth," "Prophet," and "False Prophet" in a Bible dictionary.
2. Read I Corinthians 12-14.

---

[1] Many scholars think "hereby" refers only to the statement in the first part of verse 6. See NEB.

[2] If "spirit" is taken as a metonym for "prophet," the sense of the statement may be expressed: "By this we come to know the prophet of truth and the prophet of error," that is, the true prophet and the false prophet.

CHAPTER SEVEN

The Splendors of Love

(1 John 4:7—5:3a)

Robert Law expresses the opinion that within these verses I John "rises to its sublimest height." Its sentences, he says, are "sentences of gold pure and unadorned. Brief as the paragraph is [he refers specifically to 4:7-12], it is worthy to be set beside the Prologue to the Fourth Gospel, as the loftiest that man has ever been inspired to indite" (pp. 246-47).

Robertson likens the passage to I Corinthians 13. "Paul's chapter," he says, "is like a perfect prose poem while John's is like a diamond turned round and round for different angles of light to flash upon it" (quoted by Ross, p. 20).

Love has been the motif of two earlier passages in this epistle: 2:7-17, where it is represented as the great commandment which one in fellowship with God will keep; and 3:11-24, where it is shown to be the mark of likeness to the Father which God's children must bear. In the present passage, where love is introduced for the last time, it is presented as a disposition of life which has its origin in God's own nature.

Here, in the best-known and best-loved portion of the entire epistle, love finds its richest and fullest development. Counting both its verbal and substantive forms the word "love" occurs approximately forty-six times in I John. No fewer than thirty-two of these occurrences are in the passage before us. The love of God for man, of man for God, and of man for his brother are all developed.

There were three basic words for love in the Greek language: *philia, eros,* and *agape.* The first of these, which denoted affection or friendship between kindred spirits, occurs only once in the New Testament (Jas. 4:4). The cognate verb (*phileo*), which is found more frequently, is used of the love of family (Matt. 10:37), God's love for the Son (John 5:20), Christ's love for Lazarus (John 11:3), God's love for His people (John 16:27), man's love for Christ (I Cor. 16:22), and so forth.

Eros, though occasionally used in a higher sense, essentially denoted sexual desire. N. Alexander describes *eros* as "self-centered and grasping, seeking its own satisfaction by acquiring some desired object." Its object, he explains, "is always *desired because conceived to be good* and worth possessing" (p. 94). *Eros* does not appear in the New Testament.

Agape, which is the most common word for love in the New Testament (and the term used in the present passage), was practically unknown in non-biblical Greek. Trench speaks of it as "a word born within the bosom of revealed religion" and explains that "there is no trace of it in any heathen writer whatever" (p. 43). The related verb (*agapao*) was used, but it was, in classical writers, a rather cold and colorless word meaning "to esteem" or "to have regard for." There was no thought of affection nor of self-giving in it.

In the Septuagint *agape* is still not a great and distinctive word, but it is used in Wisdom 3:9 for the love of God and in Wisdom 6:18 for the love of wisdom. It remained for the apostles to give to *agape* a beauty, a richness, and a depth of meaning all its own.

Barclay explains that *agape* love "is not simply an emotion which rises unbidden in our hearts; it is a principle by which we deliberately live. *Agape* has supremely to do with the will. . . . [It] is a deliberate principle of the mind" (*More New Testament Words,* p. 15). N. Alexander describes *agape* as "spontaneous, self-giving and *indifferent to the merit of the object loved.*" He quotes Caird to the effect that *"Eros* is all take; *Philia* is give-and-take; *Agape* is all give" (p. 94).

The verses before us do not lend themselves to the kind of analysis one might make of a Pauline passage. The apostle simply looks at love from various angles, describes its many splendors, and earnestly commends its practice to us. In Findlay's words, "He holds it up as a jewel to the sun; each turn of expression, like another facet, flashes out some new ray of heavenly light" (p. 327).

The passage divides itself around four ideas: love and its grounds (4:7-12), love and the indwelling of God (4:13-16), love and its perfection (4:17—5:1), and love and obedience (5:2-3a).

I. LOVE AND ITS GROUNDS (4:7-12)

"Love one another," which runs through this paragraph like a refrain, is mentioned as the substance of an earnest appeal (verse 7), as the expression of an imperative duty (verse 11), and as the visible evidence of the indwelling of God (verse 12). Connected with each occurrence of the phrase are statements relating to the motives or grounds for mutual love.

1. *The appeal for love* (verses 7-10). John sets forth his appeal in tender yet urgent language: *Beloved, let us love one another* (verse 7a). Plummer cites the tradition preserved by Jerome that "when the Apostle became so infirm that he could not preach he used to be carried to church and content himself with the exhortation, 'Little children, love one another.'" When his hearers wearied of it and asked him why he urged this duty so constantly, he replied, "Because it is the Lord's command, and if only this be done, it is enough" (p. xxxv).

John gives two reasons for the carrying out of this appeal. One is that *love is of God* (verse 7b); the other is that *God is love* (verse 8b). The two things, however, are not to be sharply distinguished. One runs into the other. (The reader should compare the punctuation of verses 7 and 8 in KJV with the punctuation used in the NEB.)

(1) *Because love is of God* (verses 7-8a). This is taken by some interpreters to mean that love belongs to God, that it is uniquely His property. But it is better to see in the words an affirmation that love, *agape* love, has its origin and source in God. It is therefore a distinctive aspect of His being and flows forth from Him as light radiates from the sun. This being the case, the presence of love in one's life is an evidence that he is a Christian. As John puts it, *Every one that loveth is born of God, and knoweth* [is acquainted with] *God* (verse 7b).

The opposite of this is also true. *He that loveth not knoweth not God* (verse 8a). The NEB: "but the unloving know nothing of God." As Plummer says, "Not to have known love is not to have known God" (p. 100).

The tense of the word translated "knoweth" (past [aorist], not present) is significant. The thought is that the unloving person has not once known God, regardless of professions to the contrary. If love is not now the controlling principle of his life, then not only does he not now know God, he has never known him. He "has never had in him even the beginnings of knowledge of God" (Alford, p. 1739).

The reader should take note of the fact that John does not say, "He that loveth not *knoweth nothing about God*." The gnostics against whom he was writing may have known many things *about* God; the point John makes is that they did not know God. There is a vast difference between knowing about God and actually knowing God.

(2) *Because God is love* (verses 8b-10). The assertion that "God is love" is stronger than the preceding one concerning the divine origin of love. Indeed, this brief sentence, stated twice in this paragraph (cf. verse 16), is one of the most profound and most meaningful of the whole Bible. (Compare "God is spirit," John 4:24; "God is light," I John 1:5.)

"God is love" suggests that love is such a necessity of God's nature, such an integral part of His very essence, that He cannot exist without loving. Love never is or can be absent from His being. It is to be observed, however, that the construction of the Greek is such as to make clear that love does not express all there is to the being of God. God is love, but we cannot say that love is God.

Dodd rightly points out that "God is love" is more than an assertion that "God loves." The latter, which might stand alongside such statements as "God creates," "God rules," "God judges," simply affirms that love is one of God's activities. But to assert that "God is love" is to say that love is of the very essence of God, that all His activity, therefore, is loving activity. If He creates, He creates in love; if He rules, He rules in love; if He judges, He judges in love. All that He does is the expression of His nature, which is to love.

The theologians rightly remind us that God's love is not merely amiable good will; it is holy love. God's love, therefore, never operates in a fashion contrary to His righteousness. It never moves Him to do that which would violate His own holy law.

Verses 9 and 10 bring out two things: (1) how we know that

God is love and (2) the greatness of His love. Concerning the first of these, John tells us we know that God is love because of what He has done: *Herein was the love of God manifested in us, that God hath sent his only begotten Son into the world that we might live through him* (verse 9, ASV). "Herein" looks forward to the clause beginning "that God. . . ." The "love·of God" is God's love for us. "Manifested" means "disclosed," "brought to light," "made visible." The point of the entire statement, therefore, is that the sending of God's Son into the world was the means whereby God made His love visible to us.

This manifestation of God's love was made "in us." (The KJV translates it "toward us" and construes the phrase with "love of God" [cf. NEB, TEV, TCNT]. The ASV, which seems to give a better rendering of the Greek, construes it with the verb "manifested.") The Greek might be translated "in our case," "in regard to us," or "among us" (RSV). Other manifestations of divine love had been given in Old Testament times, but John knew that the supreme revelation of that love had been given "among us."

"Hath sent," a perfect tense, emphasizes the abiding results of Christ's mission in the world.

The greatness of the divine love is indicated in at least four ways: First, it is seen in the greatness of the gift which love prompted God to bestow on us: "his only begotten Son." Nowhere else in the epistle does John use this full title. In other places he speaks of "the Son," "his Son," or "the Son of God." The emphasis, therefore, is not simply upon the fact that God sent Jesus, "but that Jesus, who was sent, is God's Only-Begotten Son" (Law, p. 73). "He calls him his *only-begotten,*" writes Calvin, "for the sake of amplifying. For in this he more clearly shewed how singularly he loved us, because he exposed his only Son to death for our sakes" (p. 239).

"Only begotten" is not applied to Christ outside of the writings of John, where it occurs five times (John 1:14, 18; 3:16, 18; I John 4:9). The only other occurrences of the word are in Hebrews 11: 17, where it is used of Isaac, Abraham's "only begotten son"; in Luke 7:12, of the "only son" of the widow of Nain; in Luke 8:42, of Jairus' "only daughter"; and in Luke 9:38, of an "only child."

Most scholars feel that the word is best translated "only." They argue that the primary idea in it is uniqueness. Christ is God's Son in a sense in which no one else is or can be Son of God.

It was the sending of such a Son, one so dear to the Father, that proved the magnitude of His love for sinful men. As Stott comments, "No greater gift of God is conceivable because no greater gift was possible" (p. 162). And Law writes that "it is His own bleeding heart the Father lays on Love's altar, when He offers His Only-Begotten Son" (p. 74).

Second, the greatness of the divine love is seen in the purpose of the Son's mission: "that we might live through him." The tense of "live" suggests the rendering, "that we might *come to have life* through him." The NEB: "to bring us life." The statement is reminiscent of "should not perish but have everlasting life" (John 3:16).

Third, the greatness of God's love is brought out by a consideration of the recipients of His love: *Herein is love, not that we loved God, but that he loved us* (verse 10a). Law thinks the meaning is that real love, love in its essence, is not revealed in our love to God but in His love to us. "The Apostle does not say that we have not loved God. What he says is that we *have* loved God, but that this is not love to call love [i.e., it is hardly worthy of the name]. That we have loved God is nothing wonderful. The ineffable mystery of Love reveals itself in this, that God has loved us, who are so unworthy of His Love, and so repulsive to all the sensibilities . . . of His moral nature" (p. 75).

Calvin, who is representative of the more traditional interpretation of this verse, thinks the meaning is that although we did *not* love God, God loved us. The apostle "meant by these words to teach us that God's love toward us has been gratuitous. . . . God freely loved us . . . because he loved us before we were born, and also when, through depravity of nature, we had hearts turned away from him" (p. 240).

Fourth, the greatness of God's love is seen in the propitiatory character of Christ's death. God sent His Son *to be the propitiation for our sins* (verse 10b). The words point up that God's love is a costly, self-sacrificing love for sinners. "As a father drinks a full cup of sorrow and humiliation in striving to make atonement for the criminal profligacies of an unworthy son, even so, Almighty God, in the person of His Son, humbles Himself and suffers unto blood for the sins of His creatures" (Law, p. 74).

As indicated earlier (on 2:2), "propitiation" suggests that there was something in the nature of God that required the sacrifice of Christ on the cross if we were to be saved. This verse makes it quite clear that the same God whose righteous nature required a sacrifice is the God whose love provided that sacrifice.

2. *The obligation to love* (verse 11). In verse 11 John returns to the thought of reproducing God's love in our own lives (cf. verse 7). There is, however, a slight difference in the statements of verses

7 and 11. Verse 7 is an exhortation: "Let us love one another." Verse 11 is not an exhortation, but the statement of a fact: *Beloved, if God so loved us, we* [emphatic] *also ought to love one another* (ASV).

The key word in verse 11 is "ought." Used twice already in this epistle (2:6; 3:16), it is a very strong term expressing moral obligation. "We are bound" conveys something of its meaning.

John enforces the thought of our obligation to love by pointing to the matchless love of God for us: "If God so loved us, we ought also to love one another." His love supplies the incentive, the motivation, and the example for ours. Conner has written: "If we do not love one another, we are not making the response to the love of God that we ought. If God's love were only an abstract proposition without definite evidence to substantiate it, then the obligation to love on our part would not be so definite. But in response to such definite love manifested in what the Son of God did for us, there is a definite and inescapable obligation on our part to love one another" (p. 63).

In the phrase "so loved," identical with the phrase used in John 3:16, the stress is on "so." The idea is both quantitative (so much) and qualitative (in such a manner), but the emphasis is on the latter. God's self-giving love was drawn forth by our need, not by any good within us, and it found in our sin the occasion for its fullest expression.

3. *The function of love* (verse 12). The kind of love John is discussing fulfills two functions in our lives. First, it is the visible evidence that God dwells in us. *No man hath seen God at any time. If we love one another, God dwelleth in us* (verse 12a).

The connection of thought in this verse is obscure. It may be this: Even though no one has ever seen God, when we love one another, and are thus in spiritual accord with God, God is in us as really as if we saw Him. Wherever His love is, God is (Sawtelle). Or, the sense may be as follows: Since God is invisible, we cannot manifest our love to Him in the usual ways. He does not need human beneficence and sacrifice. If we suppose that we love God, leaving man aside, our love is a sheer delusion. Our love for God reaches Him only when it is expressed through love for our neighbors (Ramsay). Or, there may be the suggestion here that the living of a life of love is the means of letting the invisible God be seen. That is to say, the only way in which the people of this world can ever see God is as they see Him living in and through His people. In a statement remarkably similar to this in his gospel (1:18) John teaches that it is Christ who has declared the invisible God. But here, to our astonishment, he teaches that "the unseen God, who was once revealed in His Son, is now revealed in His people if and when they love one another" (Stott, p. 164).

"Hath seen" translates a verb which means to gaze upon or to contemplate. The Greek word for "God" is without the article, which means that the emphasis of the word is qualitative: no man has ever gazed upon the essence of deity, "God as God" (Law). Mortal eyes simply cannot look upon deity (cf. Exod. 33:20).

Second, when we practice love, *his* [God's] *love is perfected in us* (verse 12b). "His love" is understood by some to mean our love for God (cf. Moffatt), but the context favors the view that it is God's love for us. "Is perfected" means essentially "has been brought to a proper end." The thought then is this: When we as Christians practice love for one another, it is an evidence that the goal of God's love has been reached in us. "Brotherly love is God's love fulfilling its ends and bearing fruit" (Sawtelle).

II. LOVE AND THE INDWELLING OF GOD (4:13-16)

The two thoughts with which the foregoing paragraph closed, the indwelling of God and the perfection of love, are now given fuller treatment — the divine indwelling in verses 13-16 and the perfection of love in 4:17—5:1.

Many commentaries see this paragraph as a discussion of the relation of love and belief (cf. Law and Ramsay), but the idea of the divine indwelling is so prominently featured (verses 13, 15, 16) that it must be understood as the central concept. Love, though not mentioned until verse 16 is reached, is brought in as a sort of crowning evidence of the believer's living union with God.

1. *The gift of the Spirit as an evidence of God's indwelling* (verse 13). Verse 13, which closely parallels 3:24b, affirms that the presence of the Spirit within us certifies the indwelling of God: *This is how we are sure that we live in God and he lives in us: he has given us his Spirit* (TEV). The thought is closely connected with that of verse 12. There we are told that the invisible God is revealed to others as they see Him in our loving deeds. Here we are taught that He gives *us* a witness of His presence. The general sense is that "the Spirit in our hearts is the seal and·assurance of our union with God" (Sawtelle, p. 51).

W. Alexander quotes Augustine: "Whence know we then that He hath given us from His Spirit? Ask your own heart. If it is full of love, you have the Spirit. Whence know we that you may thus

know that the Spirit dwelleth in you? Ask St. Paul (Rom. v. 5)"
p. 335).

2. *The confession that Jesus is the Son of God as an evidence of
God's indwelling* (verses 14-15). The first of these verses sets forth
the apostolic testimony to the Son and His saving mission to the
world: *And we have beheld and bear witness that the Father hath
sent the Son to be the Saviour of the world* (ASV). The verse following (15) states that the acknowledgment of the truth of this
testimony is an evidence of one's living union with God: *Whosoever
shall confess that Jesus is the Son of God, God abideth in him, and he
in God* (ASV).[1]

Several items in verse 14 call for consideration. For one thing,
the verse stresses that the apostolic faith was based on first-hand information. The pronoun ("we"), which refers to John and others
who were eyewitnesses of the life of Christ on earth, is emphatic
("we on our part"). The NEB: "we have seen for ourselves."

Again, there is emphasis on the content of the apostolic witness:
"that the Father hath sent the Son to be the Saviour of the world."
This witness was not a mere recital of facts, but of facts with their
interpretation. The essence of it is that Jesus is God's Son, that He
was in the world on a mission for the Father, and that that mission
concerned the salvation of the world (cf. John 4:42).

"Have beheld," which betokens an attentive, contemplative
look, is used for the second time within this paragraph (cf. verse 12).
In the earlier verse it was declared that no man has ever looked
upon God. This verse, with obvious allusion to that declaration, asserts that the God whom men had never seen did make it possible for
the apostles and their contemporaries to behold Him (in the person
of His Son).[2]

The tenses of the verbs are significant. "Have beheld" is per-

---

[1] We are interpreting verses 14 and 15 as expressing related thoughts (cf.
paragraphing of TCNT). Many scholars, however, see verse 14 as more closely
related to the thought of the verse which precedes it (cf. Moffatt's punctuation).
Stott summarizes it: "Christian certainty rests both on the objective historical
fact of the Son's mission and on the subjective inward experience of the Spirit's
witness. Another way of putting it is that there are two witnesses — the
apostles (14) and the Holy Spirit (13)" (p. 166).

[2] Calvin interprets the "beholding" as that which "belongs to faith, by which
they recognized the glory of God in Christ, according to what follows, that
he was *sent* to be the *Saviour of the world;* and this knowledge flows from
the illumination of the Spirit" (p. 243). Thus he sees an intimate relation
between the thought of verse 13 and that of verse 14. Specifically, he takes
verse 14 to be an amplification of the work of the Spirit alluded to in verse 13.

fect, suggesting that their vision of Christ had produced lasting results in their lives. W. Alexander paraphrases it: "We have seen with adoring wonder — and the impression of the sight abides with us" (p. 335). "Bear witness" is present, indicating habitual action. "Hath sent," another perfect tense, suggests the continuing consequences of the Son's mission to the world. The mission itself is in the past, but its influence and effects are still present.

Now consider verse 15. Having affirmed the apostolic testimony to Christ in verse 14, John here draws a conclusion: "Whosoever shall confess that Jesus is the Son of God [the burden of the apostolic testimony set out in the preceding verse], God abideth in him, and he in God" (verse 15, ASV). In context this statement suggests that confession is a part of the plan by which Christ, who potentially is Savior of the world, becomes one's Savior actually.

The essence of the confession is an acknowledgment of Jesus as the eternal Son of God (cf. 4:2 and II John 7). This, however, is far more than the recital of a creed. Calvin expresses the view that John uses faith and confession as interchangeable ideas. And Barker reminds us that "to confess Jesus as Messiah and Son of God was a costly act in the first century A.D.; it sundered from the nation of the Jews and from the social life of paganism. That 'confession' would only be made by one who knew Jesus Christ as an indwelling power to whom absolute loyalty was due, and who made that absolute loyalty a possibility" (p. 69).

"Shall confess," which translates an aorist tense, points to "a single and decisive public confession, the time of which is unspecified" (Stott, p. 167). The RSV renders it "confesses"; the NEB, "acknowledges."

3. *Abiding in love as an evidence of God's indwelling* (verse 16). This verse continues John's personal testimony. *And we know and have believed the love which God hath in us* (ASV). The first person pronoun ("we") refers (as in verse 14) to John and others like him who had been eyewitnesses of our Lord's ministry. (Alford, Smith, and others, however, do not limit the pronoun in this manner. They see it as including John and his readers.)

"We know" and "have believed" are both perfect tenses. "We have come to know (and still know) and we have come to believe (and still believe)" is the meaning. The knowledge and the faith are both lasting experiences. The joining of the two words here suggests the intimate relation of spiritual knowledge and belief. Calvin, who translates it "We have known by believing," explains that "such knowledge is not attained but by faith" (p. 244).

"In us" may mean "in regard to us" or "in our case." The RSV and other recent versions read "for us."

In the latter part of verse 16 John repeats the profound declaration that *God is love* (cf. verse 8) and from this draws the conclusion that *he that abideth in love abideth in God, and God abideth in him* (ASV). The apostle indicates that it is not enough merely to know that God is love. Those who profess to know this should themselves abide in love, for only those who abide in love truly abide in God and have God abiding in them. Stott explains: "The apostle does not mean that the way to come to dwell in God and He in us is to confess Christ's divine sonship (15) and to abide in love (16), but the reverse. It is the divine indwelling which alone makes possible both belief and love. They are its fruit, and therefore its evidence" (p. 168).

III. LOVE AND ITS PERFECTION (4:17—5:1)

Earlier, in verse 12, the apostle affirmed that if we love one another God dwells in us and His love is perfected in us. The thought of the indwelling of God was reflected upon in verses 13-16; now John elaborates on the idea of love and its perfection. There is this difference, however. In verse 12 the perfection of love had to do with the perfection of God's love for us. Here it is the perfection of our love that is meant.

The key expression is found in verse 17: *Herein is love made perfect with us* (ASV). John does not mean by this that any one of us loves perfectly. In love, as in all else, only God is perfect. Rather, he had in mind the ripened fruit of love. That is to say, when love is properly developed in our lives, it will bring forth certain fruit. Two things are mentioned: boldness in the day of judgment (4:17-18), and love for our Christian brothers (4:19—5:1).

1. *Boldness in the day of judgment* (verses 17-18). It is debatable whether "herein" of verse 17 is prospective or retrospective. N. Alexander interprets the word as retrospective. That is to say, he sees this verse as teaching that in God's abiding in us and our abiding in God, love finds its consummation; as a result of this, we have absolute confidence in the day of judgment. Barclay, on the other hand, sees it as prospective. That is to say, he understands the verse to teach that love finds its peak in this fact, namely, that we have full confidence on judgment day. Either interpretation is possible, though the latter is perhaps to be preferred.

The word translated *boldness* occurs here for the third time in the epistle (cf. 2:28; 3:21). As explained elsewhere, it basically means freedom of speech and then in a general way bold, fearless confidence. Here it is represented as an evidence that our love has been perfected.

The day of judgment is the day at the end of the age when all men shall give account of themselves to God.

In the latter part of verse 17, John explains how such boldness is possible on judgment day. It is *because as he is, even so are we in this world* (ASV). The primary reference in these words is to our standing, our position, before God. That is to say, in this world our standing before God is the same as the standing of our glorified Lord. We are accepted in Him (Eph. 1:6) and may share His confidence toward the Father.

Brooke sees in these words an allusion to our sharing in the character of Christ. "Those who are like their Judge, can await with confidence the result of His decrees" (p. 124).

John proceeds to explain that *There is no fear in love* (verse 18). The NEB: "There is no room for fear in love." "Fear," which is obviously used here in the sense of dread or terror, is the opposite of bold confidence. *Perfect love,* writes John, *casteth out fear, because fear hath punishment* (ASV). In a general sense this means that love and fear are mutually exclusive; and this is because fear implies punishment, a thing utterly alien to love. So if fear is present, it is evidence that perfected love is absent. "Till fear has been 'cast outside,' love has not been made perfect" (Brooke, p. 125).

"Fear hath punishment" may mean only that fear is associated with punishment. The RSV: "fear has to do with punishment." Or, it may mean that there is punishment in fear. As Brooke puts it, fear has "in itself something of the nature of punishment" (p. 125). The former interpretation is to be preferred.

2. *Loving concern for our brothers* (4:19—5:1). The second fruit of perfected love (i.e., love for God) is love for our fellow Christians. Verse 19 states this in terms of a principle: *We love, because he* [God] *first loved us* (ASV). Love, not fear, is that which marks God's people. And their love is in response to God's love. Or, to put it another way, their capacity to love comes from Him.

Beginning at 4:20 and continuing through 5:1 John tells why love for God must express itself in love for our brothers. Three reasons are given:

(1) *A matter of opportunity* (verse 20). The point of this

verse is not that men are more amiable than God, but that men afford us the opportunity of demonstrating in an objective way the reality of our love for God. As Law writes, "Visibility and invisibility signify the presence or absence, not of attraction or incitement to love, but of opportunity for loving. . . . In the nature of the case there is no other medium through which our love to God . . . can be realised than by loving our brother" (p. 252). Brooke explains that love must find an object, and "if it fails to find out the nearer object [our fellows] it will never reach the further [God]" (pp. 125-26).

(2) *A matter of obedience* (verse 21). This verse asserts that love of our brothers is not optional. God's command is not simply that we love Him, but that we love our brother also. Therefore, one who fails to love His brother does not fail merely in an obligation to the brother; he fails to obey a positive command of God. Ross writes that "love is not an emotion to which we may give expression now and then, as we feel inclined; it is a duty required of us at all times by God, and the children of God ought surely to obey their Heavenly Father" (p. 208).

(3) *A matter of family feeling* (5:1).[3] This verse is an expansion upon the statement of 4:21. That verse tells of God's command that we love our brother. This verse explains who our brother is. The gist of the whole verse is: "The children of God are those who believe that Jesus is the Christ; and everyone who loves a father loves also his children."

To believe *that Jesus is the Christ* is to accept as fact the identity of the man Jesus with the divine Christ who became incarnate in Him. It is tantamount to believing that Jesus is the Son of God (cf. discussion of 2:22).

Everyone who thus believes *is begotten of God* (ASV). This is the fifth occurrence of the Greek word rendered "is begotten" (2:29; 3:9, twice; 4:7). Weymouth expresses the meaning: "Everyone who believes that Jesus is the Christ is a child of God."

The apostle does not actually say whether faith is the cause or the consequence of the new birth, but the tenses suggest that believing is subsequent to the new birth. As Spurgeon says, "Faith in the living God and His Son Jesus Christ is always the result of

---

[3]There is no sharp division between chapters 4 and 5; the opening verses of the latter serve in one sense as a conclusion to the discussion of love and in another sense as the beginning of a new section on faith. However, it seems to the present writer that love (mentioned five times) is more prominent than faith (mentioned only once).

the new birth, and can never exist except in the regenerate" (p. 579). The stress in this passage, however, is on the fact that the two things go together.

And whosoever loveth him that begat loveth him also that is begotten of him (ASV). This states the principle that a child's love for his parent carries with it love for the parents' other children. "Since God regenerates us by faith, he must necessarily be loved by us as a Father; and this love embraces all his children" (Calvin, p. 250).

"Him that begat" is clearly a reference to God, but opinions differ as to the reference in "him that is begotten of him." Some feel that it is Christ who is meant. Weymouth, for instance, renders it, "and every one who loves the Father loves Him who is the Father's Child." Most interpreters, however, take these words as the statement of a general principle. The NEB: "and to love the parent means to love his child."

IV. LOVE AND OBEDIENCE (5:2-3a)

Verse 2 shows that true love of one's brothers is grounded in love for God and obedience to His commands: *Hereby we know that we love the children of God, when we love God and do his commandments* (ASV). Love for God is demonstrated by showing love for one's brothers (4:2—5:1), but the converse is also true. Love for God (expressed in obedience to His commands) is an evidence that we truly love the children of God. "The highest service that any man can render to humanity is to 'love God and keep His commandments'" (Law, p. 254).

Verse 3a is a further development of the relation of love for God and obedience to His commands. Goodspeed conveys the force of it: "Loving God means obeying his commands." The NEB: "to love God is to keep his commands." Where there is no obedience to God there is no love for God. The two are inseparable.[4]

FOR FURTHER STUDY

1. Read I John and mark every occurrence of the word "love."
2. Note the uses of the word "perfect" in I John.

---

[4]It should be noticed that in 5:1-3 John's three principal tests of spiritual life — belief, love, and righteousness — are brought together in such a way as to show that if any one of them is lacking the absence of eternal life is to be inferred.

CHAPTER EIGHT

The Faith That Conquers

(1 John 5:3b-12)

The concept of faith is peculiarly prominent in the Johannine writings. Indeed, more than half of the one hundred occurrences of the verb "believe" in the New Testament are found in the writings of John. Oddly enough, however, the noun "faith" is found only once in all the Johannine literature. That one occurrence is in the present passage (verse 4).

Law calls attention to the fact that John, unlike other New Testament writers, commonly makes the object of the verb "believe" a fact or a proposition, rather than a person. In John, then, "believing" regularly denotes "the perception of a truth or the crediting of a testimony" rather than "the action of the will in trust and self-committal." To put it another way, in John "believing" is "less frequently a direct personal relation to Christ, more frequently a theological conception of Christ" (pp. 258-259). It is, then, not to be sharply distinguished from confession, an idea which is also prominent in this epistle.

In earlier portions of I John "belief" has been mentioned only four times (3:23; 4:1, 16; 5:1). In those references we are taught that belief in the name of the Son and love for one another are God's "commandment" for His people (3:23), that we are not to give credence to every prophetic utterance but are to test each for authenticity (4:1), that we have come to know and have believed

God's love for us (4:16), and that belief in Christ is the mark of the new birth (5:1).

In the present passage (5:3b-12) the occurrences of the idea of belief ("believe," four times; "faith," once) are more numerous than are its occurrences in all the preceding chapters of the epistle. Here we learn of faith's conquering power (verses 3b-5), faith's personal object (verse 6), and faith's authenticating witnesses (verses 7-12).

I. FAITH'S CONQUERING POWER (verses 3b-5)

The last part of verse 3 seems to be more closely related to what follows (verse 4a) than it is to what precedes it (verse 3a). (See the punctuation of NEB.) Verse 3b states a fact: *His commandments are not grievous.* Verse 4a explains why this is so: *for whatever is born of God conquers the world* (Moffatt).

In the statement "his commandments are not grievous" the idea is not that God's requirements are not exacting; experience teaches that they are profoundly exacting. The meaning is that God's commands are not burdensome (RSV) or irksome (Weymouth).

If we follow the punctuation of KJV, ASV, RSV, and others, the main idea is that love keeps God's commands from becoming an oppressive burden. The punctuation of NEB stresses the idea that it is God's work in us (the new birth) which keeps the divine commands from becoming an oppressive burden. Perhaps both ideas are present. As Ramsay explains it, "Love makes obedience easy, and the life of God in the soul makes obedience possible" (p. 316).

The statement that "whatsoever is begotten of God overcometh the world" (verse 4a) requires explanation. "Whatsoever" (verse 4), a neuter construction, is particularly significant. For one thing, it is more comprehensive than the masculine "whosoever." It states the matter as a broad principle: Whatever is begotten of God has in it a conquering element that sweeps all difficulties out of the way. Sawtelle remarks that "the conflict will be great sometimes, and the world is not subdued at once; nevertheless, the new nature goes on to victory, and overcomes wholly in the end. For it is like God" (p. 55).

Furthermore, the neuter, which is collective and generalizing in force, emphasizes not so much the persons who conquer but the divine life by which they conquer. (Compare 4:4, where the Christian's victory is attributed to the fact that "he that is in you" is greater than "he that is in the world.")

"Overcometh," a present tense, suggests two things: (1) that the Christian's conflict with the world is still in progress, and (2) that continuous victory is possible.

"The world" here, as nearly always in John's epistle, stands for all of the forces and powers of evil pitted against God and His people. Calvin defines it as "whatever is adverse to God's Spirit," including "the depravity of our nature."

In verse 4b the victory over the world is specifically attributed to the Christian's faith: *And this is the victory that overcometh the world, even our faith.* The Greek text contains a play on words which cannot easily be reproduced in an English translation. Moffatt's "the conquest which conquers the world" is an attempt to do so. Perhaps, as John Owen suggests, the Greek word for "victory" (*nike*) is personified: "And this is the conqueress who conquers the world, even our faith" (footnote in Calvin, p. 254). (In Greek mythology *nike* was the name of the goddess of victory.)

"Overcometh," a past tense (aorist) in Greek, is more accurately rendered "hath overcome" (ASV), or simply "overcame." The significance of the tense — compare the present tense of the same verb in the first half of the verse — is not altogether obvious. The apostle may have chosen the aorist tense as a way of referring to (pinpointing) the initial victory won by the Christian in his conversion. Ross, however, would not limit it to the initial experience. He feels that John was reminding his readers of the many occasions in the past when their faith overcame the world. (Compare Law, who, observing that the aorist tense does not necessarily refer to a definite point in the past, expresses the view that in this passage the tense is "constative"; that is, that it sums up the whole action in one view, reduces it to a point.) D. Smith thinks the past tense is used in order to emphasize that though the conflict is not over, the victory is assured. Brooke, who takes an entirely different approach, prefers to interpret the word as a reference to the victory of the Asian Christians over their gnostic opponents (cf. 2:19; 4:4).

"Our faith" is equated with victory over the world, though in reality faith is the *means* by which the victory is won. (The construction, therefore, is an example of metonymy.) Alford explains that "the identifying of the victory with the faith which gained it is a concise and emphatic way of linking the two inseparably together, so that wherever there is faith there is victory" (p. 1747). The general thought is that our faith is that by which we lay hold on the power of God. It is therefore the spiritual weapon by which temptation is met and overcome.

Verse 5 does two things: First, it reiterates the vital role which faith plays in the conquest of the world. Second, it defines the faith that conquers. The verse is so worded that it constitutes a sort of challenge to the readers to produce a single instance of victory over the world that has not come by faith. In effect, the writer asks: If there are any besides believers who have vanquished this godless world, where are they? The indication is that the person to whom victory belongs is in every case the person who believes *that Jesus is the Son of God*. These last words point up the substance of conquering faith, namely, that the man Jesus is the incarnate Son of God. He, though apparently overwhelmed by defeat and disaster, overcame the world and became the source of all-conquering power to His people (John 16:33).

II. FAITH'S PERSONAL OBJECT (verse 6)

The closing portion of verse 5 has indicated that faith concerns Jesus, the Son of God. The personal name, "Jesus," calls to mind His real humanity. "Son of God," the divine title, points to His true deity. The form of the statement, "that Jesus is the Son of God," emphasizes the union of humanity and deity in the one person.

Verse 6 is intended to give a more precise description of Jesus, the Son of God: *This is he that came by water and blood, even Jesus Christ* (verse 6a). Here it is to be observed that the One with whom our faith has to do is designated in two ways. We may notice first that He is called "Jesus Christ." This name is an exact equivalent of "Jesus the Son of God," for John uses the term "Christ" interchangeably with the title "Son of God." The two words, then, pick up and repeat the closing words of verse 5, "that Jesus is the Son of God."

In addition, Jesus Christ is designated as "he that came." Some scholars understand these words to be an allusion to the terms "he that cometh" and "he that came," which are used in the gospels as technical designations of the Messiah (cf. Matt. 11:3; 23:39; John 3:31; 6:14; 11:27; 12:13, *et al.*). Viewed in this manner, "he that came" may be practically equivalent to a messianic title. Brooke, on the other hand, thinks we are not justified in reading this much into the phrase. He feels that it points up the character of Christ's work and interprets it to mean "He who accomplished the Mission entrusted to Him by God" (p. 135).

Furthermore, Christ is described as He who came "by water and blood." These terms will be repeated in verse 8 and will be identified as part of a threefold witness to Jesus Christ. It is worthy of notice, however, that the idea of witness is not actually mentioned in this verse. Here the water and the blood are represented as historical realities in the mission of the Son of God. The tense of "came" (aorist) suggests that "water" and "blood" refer to events in the life of Jesus in which He was revealed to be the Son of God.

Law explains that the obscurity of this verse is doubtless due to the fact that the first readers of the epistle were so familiar with its terminology that John did not feel it necessary to explain what he meant. "The water" and "the blood," according to Law, are "a kind of verbal shorthand, intended merely to recall to [John's] readers the exposition of those themes which they had heard from his lips" (p. 95).

The words have been variously interpreted. Some, for instance, have taken them to be references to the ordinances of baptism and the Lord's Supper. However, the use of the past tense ("came") rules out this interpretation. Others have seen in the words an allusion to the crucifixion of Christ when His pierced side gave forth both blood and water. This interpretation is highly improbable. Here we are told that Christ came "by" (or "through") water and blood. At the crucifixion the blood and the water came "out of" Him. Calvin, who interpreted the preposition ("by") to mean "with" or "accompanied by," looked upon "the water" and "the blood" as symbolizing, respectively, the cleansing and atonement brought to us by Christ.

If we are to arrive at the true interpretation, we must keep in mind the immediate background of the epistle. In particular, we must remember that John was combatting a heresy which differentiated between the man Jesus and the divine Christ. Its proponents held that Jesus was a mere man upon whom the divine Christ came at His baptism and from whom the divine Christ departed before He died. Jesus was therefore born as a man and He died as a man, but for the brief period of His ministry (begun at His baptism) the divine Christ was upon Him. This entire passage must be seen as a refutation of that heresy. In light of these facts, the most satisfactory interpretation is that which relates the water and the blood to historical events in the life and ministry of Jesus by which He "came." These events were His baptism in the Jordan River and His death on the cross.

John's opponents taught that the Christ came "by water" (the baptism) but denied that He came "by blood" (the death). This accounts for the apostle's emphatic assertion that Jesus Christ came

not with the water only, but with the water and with the blood
(ASV). It was inconceivable to the gnostics that the divine Christ
should suffer the pain and shame of Calvary. To John, what happened at the cross was the heart of the Gospel. He insisted therefore that Jesus Christ came not simply by the water of baptism (as
the gnostics taught), but by the blood of the death also (which they
denied).

Of course, the apostle does not intend to imply that before the
baptism Jesus was not the Christ, the Son of God. He emphatically
asserts that it was Jesus Christ — observe the human and the divine
name — who came by water and by blood to accomplish His mission. His point is that the eternal God was incarnate in Jesus
throughout the course of His human life.

The baptism and the death were, however, immensely important events in the carrying out of the messianic mission. As Brooke
explains "they stand out more prominently than any other two
recorded events of the Ministry" (p. 135). At His baptism Jesus
consecrated Himself to His redemptive mission, was divinely attested
by the voice from heaven, and was anointed with the Holy Spirit.
At the cross His messianic mission was consummated and His propitiatory death constituted Him the Savior.[1]

III. FAITH'S AUTHENTICATING WITNESSES[2] (verse 7-12)

The purpose of these verses is to show that our faith in Jesus
Christ is well grounded. To make his point the apostle marshals a
threefold testimony to Christ (verses 7-8) and then shows that this
testimony is in truth the testimony of God Himself to His Son (verse
9). This divine witness is then shown to be confirmed in the inner
experience of the believer (verse 10). Finally, the content or substance of the divine witness is stated in verses 11 and 12.

In the study of this paragraph, the reader should keep before
him ASV or some other modern translation, for KJV translates a

---

[1]Some interpreters explain the significance of the baptism and the death by
reference to the fact that the divine voice is associated with both these events.
See, for example, Taylor's *Living New Testament*.

[2]A distinctive feature of both the gospel of John and the first epistle is the
emphasis on "witness." In the former, counting both verb and noun forms,
the word occurs a total of forty-seven times. In I John the verb and the
noun are found six times each. With only two exceptions, all of these are
clustered in the present passage. The prominence of the idea of witness is
greatly obscured in KJV by its needless variation in translating the Greek words
("bear witness," "bear record," "testify," "witness," "record," etc.).

Greek text which has no ancient authority and is universally rejected by biblical scholars.[3]

1. *The witness of the Spirit* (verse 7, ASV). The preceding verse has taught that Jesus Christ is "he that came" (verse 6a); that is to say, He is the one who fulfills the divine plan of redemption. This verse teaches that it is the special function of the Holy Spirit to bear witness to this fact. The idea seems to be that the Spirit reveals the significance of Christ's coming and applies its truth to our hearts. Indeed, without His work, the wonder and glory of it all would be forever hidden to us. As Calvin writes, "Whatever signs of divine glory may shine forth in Christ, they would yet be obscure to us and escape our vision, were not the Holy Spirit to open for us the eyes of faith" (p. 259).

The question is sometimes raised as to when and where the Spirit gives His testimony to the Christ. Some refer to the coming of the Spirit upon Jesus at the baptism in Jordan. Others see a reference to what happened on the day of Pentecost. It is more probable, however, that the reference is to the total witness of the Holy Spirit. (Observe the present tense, "beareth witness." There may be in the statement an allusion to John 15:26.) This means that the Spirit's witness is not to be limited to the subjective witness which He bears in the heart of the believer, though that of course is a large part of it. (The inner witness is treated more specifically in verse 10.)

Barrett understands the Spirit's witness to include the new birth by which He quickens the soul, the sanctifying power which He exerts on the lives of true believers, the power with which He accompanies the faithful preaching of the Gospel, and the illumination which He sheds on the Word of God. Spurgeon, in addition to these things, speaks of the consoling, guiding, and sustaining ministries of the Spirit, and of the Spirit's work in great revivals, such as those under Luther, Calvin, Whitefield, and Wesley as a part of the Spirit's witness to the truth.

The assertion that *the Spirit is the truth* (ASV) is intended to

---

[3]The spurious words begin with "in heaven" (verse 7, KJV) and continue through "in earth" (verse 8, KJV). Biblical scholarship is unanimous in its opinion that these words did not form a part of the original text of I John. Every Greek manuscript before the fifteenth century omits them. Every ancient version of the first four centuries omits them; in fact, every version earlier than the fifteenth century omits them, except the Latin. Furthermore, no Greek father quotes the passage in discussing the doctrine of the trinity. All of this is conclusive evidence that the words are not a part of the authentic Greek text.

emphasize the trustworthiness of the Spirit's witness. His very nature is truth. Law feels that "it is because 'the Spirit is Truth' that He recognizes and reveals Christ who is the embodiment of the Truth (John 14:6)" (pp. 118-19).

2. *The witness of the water and the blood* (verse 8 ASV). Previously (verse 6) the water (Christ's baptism) and the blood (Christ's death) were mentioned as historical realities in the work of Christ. Through these He "came" in the performance of His messianic mission. The water and the blood in the present verse are cited as a part of the total witness to the divine sonship of Jesus. That witness is characterized as follows:

First, it is a threefold witness: *For there are three who bear witness, the Spirit, and the water, and the blood* (ASV). In these words there is an obvious allusion to the stipulation of the Mosaic law requiring the corroborative evidence of two or three witnesses (Deut. 17:6; cf. Matt. 18:16; John 8:17). The effect here is to underscore the trustworthiness of the witness to Jesus Christ.

Second, it is a continuing witness. The Spirit, the water, and the blood "bear witness" (present tense). Some commentators concede that in verse 6 the water and the blood are thought of as historical events in the mission of Christ, but they feel that in the present verse John was thinking of baptism and the Lord's Supper "as the permanent memorials of those great events by which Jesus was identified as the Son of God" (Ramsay, p. 321). It is to be doubted, however, that John would so quickly change the meaning of his words. We therefore conclude that both in verse 6 and in verse 8 the water and the blood are references to particular events by which Christ fulfilled His messianic mission. The latter verse (8), however, makes an advance on this thought by stressing that they are abiding witnesses to the uniqueness of Christ.

Some may wonder how the baptism and death of Jesus "bear witness" to Him. Their real value is seen when we imagine what the situation would be if neither of them had ever occurred, if Christ had begun His mission without the decisive consecration at the Jordan and if He had died quietly as other men die.

Third, it is a convergent witness: *and the three agree in one* (ASV). The Greek might literally be translated "and the three are unto one." Rotherham: "are unto one thing." The NEB: "are in agreement." The thought is that the three witnesses converge to one truth, namely, that Jesus Christ is the Son of God. Ramsay explains it in this manner: "The three witnesses bear a consentient testimony:

they converge in one. Their common witness is that Jesus baptized, crucified, is the Son of God" (p. 322).

3. *The witness of the Father* (verse 9). In this verse John explains that the threefold witness to Jesus Christ — the Spirit, the water, and the blood — is, in fact, a divine witness. That is to say, it is actually God who speaks to us in the Spirit and in the historic facts of the Gospel (the water and the blood). This therefore makes the witness the more worthy of acceptance. *If we receive* [as we do] *the witness of men, the witness of God is greater.* Brooke expresses the meaning: "If we accept the testimony of men when it satisfies the conditions of evidence required by the law, much more are we bound to accept the witness which we possess in this case, for it is witness borne by God Himself" (p. 137).

Moreover, the apostle shows that the essence of the witness is a testimony borne by a Father to His own Son: *For the witness of God is this, that he hath borne witness concerning his Son* (ASV). The point is that this is a subject on which God alone is fully competent to speak. What He says must necessarily be final, authoritative, and conclusive. His witness therefore is to be trusted implicitly.

4. *The witness of personal experience* (verse 10). To the witness of the Spirit, the witness of the water and the blood, and the witness of the Father there is now added still another attestation. It is the inward witness of personal experience: *He that believeth on the Son of God hath the witness* [i.e., the witness of God, verse 9] *in him.* The RSV: "in himself."

"Believeth on the Son of God" translates a construction which denotes reliance upon, trust in, or commitment to the Son of God. It occurs with unusual frequency in the gospel of John but is found in the epistle only here, verse 10c, and verse 13. The manner in which the phrase is used here indicates that to "believe on" the Son is virtually synonymous with "receiving" the witness of God (verse 9). As Law puts it, "By believing the testimony of God, we 'believe in' His Son" (p. 125). (Compare John 1:12, where "believing" and "receiving" are used interchangeably.)

"Hath the witness in himself" refers to the inward witness of the Spirit and means that the believer is given a profound certitude of the rightness of his decision to commit himself to Christ. In addition, there is the thought that the inward witness is a subjective confirmation of the testimony set forth in the preceding verses.

Spurgeon affirms that this inward witness involves the "*wondrous sense of change* which comes over the believer," the "*won-

drous power which goes with the word of God," and the *"deep feeling of peace* which comes to us through believing in Jesus."

In sharp contrast with the person who believes in the Son of God is *he that believeth not God* (verse 10b). The manner in which the contrast is drawn shows that not to "believe in" the Son is tantamount to not "believing" God, that is, not accepting the witness which He has given to His Son.

This is an extremely grave situation, for he who rejects God's witness *hath made him a liar* (cf. 1:10). The reason is stated in verse 10c: *because he hath not believed in the witness that God hath borne concerning his Son.* "Hath made" and "hath not believed" are both perfect tenses. They reflect a past act and a continuing state or condition. "When the crisis of choice came he refused the message: he made God a liar: he did not believe on His testimony: and the result of that decision entered into him and clings to him" (Westcott, p. 187).

5. *The content of the witness* (verses 11-12). The first of these verses teaches that the divine witness points to or consists of God's gift of eternal life through His Son. *And the witness is this, that God gave unto us eternal life, and this life is in his Son* (ASV). The TEV: "This, then, is the witness: God has given us eternal life, and this life is ours in his Son." The NEB: "is found in his Son." Thus we learn that the witness actually is twofold: (1) that God gave us eternal life, and (2) that the sole medium of this life is His Son. The verse following (12) draws a conclusion: *He that hath the Son hath the life; he that hath not the Son of God hath not the life* (ASV).

The concept of "life" or "eternal life" dominates the thought of I John. The epistle begins (1:2) and ends (5:20) with references to it, and the stated purpose of the author was to give believers assurance of possessing it (5:13). "Its predominance," writes Law, "is complete; it is the centre to which every idea in the Epistle is more or less directly related" (p. 184).

The Bible does not give a formal definition of eternal life. Law calls it the "conscious participation in the highest good for which man is made" (p. 185). Since "eternal" betokens that which has neither beginning nor end, which is not subject to change and decay, which is above time, Barclay defines eternal life as *"nothing less than the life of God himself"* (*More New Testament Words,* p. 28). This helps us to see that the reference in the term is not merely to endless life. Eternal life is this, of course. But it is vastly more than this. It is a certain kind of life, a life that is possessed only by those who have been united to God through faith in Jesus Christ. It is life, therefore, which death cannot destroy.

Three great affirmations are made concerning this life. First, it is a divine gift. God *gave* to us eternal life. It is not a reward for merit; it is a free bounty from the hand of God. The tense of "gave" (verse 11, ASV) implies a point in time when something was "given once for all" (Westcott). The reference may be either to the event of the Incarnation (by which life was communicated to men, John 10:10; I John 1:2) or to the believer's conversion (when he actually came to possess eternal life).

Second, this life is a present possession. "He that hath the Son *hath* the life."

Third, it is in God's Son. "And this life is *in his Son.*" For this reason, the man who has the Son "hath the life," and he who does not have the Son "hath not the life." As N. Alexander says, "Whatever else the 'Sonless' man has, he does not have *life.* That is beyond his grasp" (p. 124). He may, by human standards, be a good man, a good neighbor, a good parent, a good citizen; but, by the standard of the Gospel, if he has no saving union with Christ, he does not have eternal life and is not a Christian.

FOR FURTHER STUDY

1. Using a concordance, make note of the occurrences of "witness," "testimony," and "testify" in the writings of John.

2. Look up in a concordance the words "Faith" and "Believe." Read articles on them in a Bible dictionary.

3. Read an article on "Eternal Life" in a Bible dictionary.

CHAPTER NINE

Great Certainties of the Gospel

(1 John 5:13-21)

This paragraph, a sort of recapitulation of the whole epistle, incorporates some of its leading ideas and gives them a final statement. The central concept is assurance, a thought which has been especially prominent throughout the epistle.

The key word, occurring no fewer than seven times in verses 13-21, is "know." In every instance except one the word renders the Greek term *oida*. The one exception is the second occurrence of "know" in verse 20, where the Greek word is *ginosko*. Altogether these two words are found at least forty times in I John (*ginosko*, twenty-five times; *oida*, fifteen times). In a general way *ginosko* denotes "the perception through which knowledge is acquired"; *oida*, "the fact of knowledge absolutely" (Law, p. 366). The former is rendered "to know," "to get to know," "to perceive," and so on. The latter means to know intuitively, to know as a matter of fact. However, we should not always insist on rigid distinctions in the meanings of these words.

The passage begins with a statement concerning the believer's assurance of eternal life (verse 13) and his confidence in the realm of prayer (verses 14-17). This is followed by an impressive assertion of three fundamental certainties relating to the believer's holiness (verse 18), his birth from God (verse 19), and the knowledge of God made possible by the redemptive mission of

127

Christ (verse 20). The final word is an urgent appeal to the apostle's "little children" to guard themselves from idols (verse 21).

I. THE POSSESSION OF ETERNAL LIFE (verse 13)

The first certainty of faith which John mentions has to do with the Christian's possession of eternal life: *These things have I written unto you, that ye may know that ye have eternal life, even unto you that believe on the name of the Son of God* (ASV). This life, a characteristic concept in the writings of John, is both quantitative and qualitative. That is to say, it is endless in duration and spiritual (even God-like) in nature. Existing eternally in God, it was historically manifested in the coming of Christ (1:2) and becomes ours in the experience of the new birth (John 3). Jesus Christ is, as it were, the great reservoir of life and is the one who mediates it to us (5:12).

Three things are to be observed in this verse. First, it declares the purpose of the epistle: "that ye may know that ye have eternal life."[1] "Assurance," writes Conner, "is the privilege and birthright of every regenerated man. . . . One need not grope in the dark about his relationship to God. Every Christian may know and should know that he has eternal life" (p. 178). "Know" is the word which means to know absolutely, and so, in this context, denotes positive, confident assurance. Findlay explains that it "signifies an abiding conviction, resting on known facts" (p. 396).

Some emphasis is placed upon the words "even unto you that believe on the name of the Son of God" (ASV). This shows that John wanted none to claim this assurance except those who had a right to it. The counterfeit Christians, whom the apostle has opposed throughout his epistle, were ruled out by this description.

It is instructive to compare the verse before us with John 20: 31, where the purpose of the gospel is stated. There we learn that the gospel was written that its readers might have life. Here we learn that the epistle was written that its readers might *know* they have life. In this there is a hint that the gospel (written with an evangelistic purpose) was probably composed first and the epistle (written to give guidance and instruction to believers) was written later. At

---

[1]Compare 1:4, which contains another general and inclusive statement of purpose. That verse and this verse complement one another, for fulness of joy (1:4) is based upon the assurance of salvation (5:13). Indications of purpose found in other passages, such as 2:1, 12-14, 21, 26, seem to relate to specific appeals within the epistle rather than to the whole composition.

any rate, the two writings are very closely related. The epistle might even have been a companion to the gospel, a sort of covering letter for it.

Second, the verse reveals how this assurance of eternal life may be gained: *"These things have I written . . . that ye may know."* The suggestion is that the epistle contains a number of tests that can be applied to one's life to determine his true status before God. See, as examples, 2:3, 5; 3:10, 14, 18-19, 24; 5:10. These texts may be applied either to ourselves or to others.

"These things" might refer to the immediately preceding passage, but it is more probable that the reference is to the entire epistle.

Third, the verse plainly implies that one may be a believer, may have eternal life, and yet not know that he has this eternal life. That is to say, he may be truly saved and at the same time entertain doubts about his salvation.

We need always to distinguish between salvation and the *assurance* of salvation. Every believer is saved, but not every believer has the assurance that he is saved. His doubts concerning this matter may arrest his spiritual growth, rob him of joy, and cripple his usefulness, but they do not alter the fact that he is saved.

II. ANSWERS TO OUR PRAYERS (verses 14-17)

Having spoken of the believer's assurance of eternal life, the apostle moves now to discuss a second assurance, that of answered prayer. The manner in which the two topics are treated signifies that assurance in prayer is a natural consequence of the assured possession of eternal life. First we must know that we are accepted with God; then, on the strength of this assurance, we have great encouragement to approach Him with our needs. (Compare 3:19-22, where there is the same deeply significant transition from a statement concerning assurance of salvation to a declaration concerning a confident approach to God in prayer.)

This brief paragraph begins with a general statement about boldness in prayer (verses 14-15) and then develops that idea with special reference to intercessory prayer (verses 16-17). We will consider its teachings under three heads: (1) our confidence in prayer (verse 14), (2) the consciousness that we have our requests (verse 15), and (3) the duty of intercessory prayer (verses 16-17).

1. *Our confidence in prayer* (verse 14). Here the apostle stresses the spirit in which the assured Christian comes before God.

And this is the boldness which we have toward him, that, if we ask anything according to his will, he heareth us (ASV). The TCNT puts it: "And this is the confidence with which we approach him, that whenever we ask anything that is in accordance with his will, he listens to us."

"Boldness" ("confidence," KJV) has occurred three times already in the epistle. Once it was used in reference to the second coming of Jesus (2:28); once, in reference to the judgment (4:17); and once (as here), in reference to prayer (3:21). The Greek term, as explained earlier, means outspokenness, freedom of speech, then bold confidence, fearless trust. Here it bespeaks the childlike confidence with which the believer approaches God. As Paul puts it, God has "sent forth the Spirit of his Son into our hearts, crying, Abba, Father" (Gal. 4:6, ASV). We can, therefore, as the writer of Hebrews says, "draw near with boldness unto the throne of grace, that we may receive mercy, and may find grace to help us in time of need" (4:16 ASV).

Opinion is divided as to the meaning of "heareth," but most commentaries understand it to include both hearing and answering (cf. John 9:21; 11:41, 42). Brooke explains that "the word naturally includes the idea of hearing favourably" (p. 144). Those who do not accept this interpretation point to "hearing" in verse 14 and "having" in verse 15, arguing that the former means listening and the latter implies granting. These two thoughts, however, seem to overlap. Either way, the burden of the statement is that the eternal God is attentive to the cries of His people. The truth is, He is far more ready to hear than we are to pray.

The one limitation to this assurance of answered prayer is that the thing requested be "according to his [God's] will" (verse 14). Elsewhere in the New Testament we are taught that prayer, to be effective, must be "in Jesus' name" (John 14:13), must proceed from a righteous life (Jas. 5:16; I John 3:22) and from unselfish motives (Jas. 4:3), must be offered in faith (Matt. 21:22; Jas. 1: 6), and so forth. "According to his will," however, seems to be the most inclusive way of setting forth the fundamental condition of effectual prayer. The statement implies that we are to recognize the infinite wisdom of God's will and subordinate our desires to it. Rightly seen, this is not a fetter to our freedom but a safeguard to it.

Law observes that "the marvellous and supernatural power of prayer consists, not in bringing God's Will down to us, but in lifting our will up to His" (p. 301). And Barclay concludes that "the ultimate test of any request is, *Can* we say to Jesus, 'Give me this for *your* sake, and in *your* name'? A prayer of which we can honestly say that will be granted" (p. 136).

2. *The consciousness that we have our requests* (verse 15). The spirit of confidence set out in the preceding verse is reiterated in slightly different words in verse 15: *and if we know that he heareth us whatsoever we ask, we know that we have the petitions that we have asked of him* (ASV). There is emphasis on "know": "If we *know* that he heareth us . . . we *know* that we have." The point is not that if God hears our requests He answers them, but that if we *know* that He hears them, we *already have*[2] (in anticipation) what we have requested in accordance with His will. Consciousness of being heard brings with it consciousness of possession.

"If we know," though a somewhat unusual construction in Greek, is not intended to express doubt or uncertainty. The assumption is that we *do* know, for this is what the preceding verse has emphatically declared.

"We have asked" (ASV) translates a perfect tense and may suggest that the petitions have been placed before the throne of grace and remain there. They are before God, and He is mindful of them.

3. *The duty of intercessory prayer* (verses 16-17). Having spoken of the efficacy of prayer generally, the apostle proceeds to speak of its efficacy in a particular direction — intercessory prayer. Such prayer is unquestionably one of the highest privileges of the Christian life, but it is also one of its most sacred responsibilities.

Verse 16a may be seen as a specific example of prayer which is in accord with God's will. *If any man see his brother sinning a sin not unto death, he shall ask, and God will give him* [the intercessor] *life for them that sin not unto death* (ASV). The thought is reminiscent of Galatians 6:1: "Even if a man should be detected in some sin, my brothers, the spiritual ones among you should quietly set him back on the right path, not with any feeling of superiority but being yourselves on guard against temptation" (Phillips; cf. James 5:19-20).

The "brother" is understood by most interpreters to be a Christian. Stott argues, but not too convincingly, that the word is used in the weakened sense of "neighbor."

The future tense in "he shall ask" may be interpreted in either of two ways. It may, for instance, have imperative force. Viewed

---

[2]The repetition of the verb "have" in verses 13-15 is worthy of notice: we have eternal life (verse 13), we have boldness toward God (verse 14), and we have the petitions that we asked of God (verse 15).

in this manner, it is the equivalent of a command for the Christian to pray for his sinning brother. On the other hand, the future tense may be used because it is assumed that the Christian will as a matter of course pray for a sinning brother. Either way, there is the suggestion that intercessory prayer is a Christian duty. In the former interpretation it is a duty commanded; in the latter, a duty assumed.

"He shall give him life" (KJV) is somewhat ambiguous. Probably the first pronoun refers to God (ASV) and the second to the intercessor, though some understand "he" to refer to the intercessor and "him" to refer to the sinning brother. The TCNT reflects this latter view: "He will ask, and so be the means of giving life to him — to any whose sin is not deadly."

Verse 16b may be seen as an example of a request which may not be according to God's will. *There is* [the verb is emphatic] *a sin unto death: not concerning this do I say that he should make request* (ASV). The NEB says: "There is such a thing as deadly sin, and I do not suggest that he should pray about that." Prayer for this person is neither commanded nor encouraged. On the other hand, it is not absolutely forbidden. The gist of the words is that where sin unto death is involved no assurance can be given that prayer will be efficacious. "Such cases lay outside the normal sphere of Christian intercession. They must be left to God alone" (Brooke, p. 147).

Two words for prayer are used in verse 16, one translated "ask," the other rendered "pray" ("make request," ASV). The former, the stronger of the two (and used also in verses 14 and 15), suggests earnest entreaty, beseeching. The latter denotes the making of a request. Though the distinction in the meanings of these two words cannot always be insisted upon, some scholars feel that the change from the one to the other is noteworthy here.

Many interpretations have been given of "sin unto death" (TEV: "sin which leads to death"). Some, for instance, understand it as *a specific act of sin,* such as murder, adultery, blasphemy, and so on. Those who take this approach see in the words an allusion to high-handed or willful sin (Num. 15:30). Others say that the reference is not to a specific act of sin, but to *a state or habit of sin* willfully chosen and persisted in. Plummer, for example, speaks of it as "constant and consummate opposition to God" (p. 123). These interpreters point to the absence of the Greek article before "sin" and emphasize that the reference is not to "a" sin unto death but to "sin unto death." (See TEV, quoted above.)

If we are to understand the nature of this sin, we must keep in mind the background of the epistle. In light of what we know of that it seems that "sin unto death" must have had primary reference to John's gnostic opponents, who had willfully rejected the Spirit's witness to the person and work of Christ. (Compare the warning concerning blasphemy against the Spirit, Luke 12:10.) But whatever the precise meaning may be, the idea is that of a kind of sinning whose natural consequence is death (spiritual ruin). "To pray for its remission," Sawtelle says, "is to pray for an impossibility. . . . It is to pray for salvation outside of Christ and the Holy Spirit" (p. 61).

Verse 17 is intended to show that sin (even that which is not unto death) is never a trivial matter.

III. VICTORY OVER SIN (verse 18)[3]

The possibility of victory over sin, which should come as wondrously glad news to all our fallen race, is the third grand assurance of our faith. The matter is stated negatively: *We know that whosoever is begotten of God sinneth not* (ASV; cf. 3:6, 9). The meaning is that the Christian's new nature makes a life of sin an utter impossibility. The thought is inserted here partly to hammer down a truth which has been a recurring emphasis in the epistle and partly to show the readers that a sinning brother (verse 16) is acting in a manner contrary to his true nature.

"We know" translates the Greek word which denotes intuitive knowledge: we know as a matter of fact. "Whosoever is begotten of God," which includes every Christian, calls attention to the divine origin of the Christian life and implies a participaton in the divine nature. "Sinneth," which translates a present tense, means that whoever is begotten of God does not habitually sin. As Plummer puts it, "A child of God may sin, but his normal condition is resistance to evil" (p. 125).

The reason for this is given in the latter part of verse 18: *but he that was begotten of God keepeth himself, and the evil one toucheth him not* (ASV). This rendering, which asserts that the believer keeps himself, puts stress upon human effort and responsibility. The RSV, following a different Greek text, offers a more attractive interpretation: "but He who was born of God keeps him, and

---

[3]Verses 18-21, which make up a single paragraph, form a resumé of the chief facts relating to the believer's new life. Most of it has to do with his union with God and the holiness which that union involves. The threefold repetition of "we know" (verses 18, 19, 20) is most impressive. So also is the solemn charge with which the letter closes (verse 21).

the evil one does not touch him." In this rendering "He who was born of God" is understood as a reference to Christ. (Observe the capital letter in "He.") The thought, then, is not that the believer keeps himself, but that Christ keeps him.

The Greek word for "keep" means to watch over so as to preserve and protect. The Christian may have "a malignant foe," but "he has also a vigilant Guardian" (D. Smith, p. 198).

Because Christ thus looks after the Christian "the evil one [Satan] toucheth him [the Christian] not" (ASV). "Toucheth" suggests getting a hold on. The evil one may indeed "touch" the believer, but he is not able to grasp him and keep him within his clutches. As Ramsay comments, "He is well kept whom Christ keeps: the enemy of souls cannot lay hold of him: he assaults but cannot seize" (p. 330). Calvin understands the statement to mean that Satan is unable to inflict "a deadly wound." The Christian, though assaulted by him, wards off his strokes by the shield of faith (p. 271).

IV. BIRTH FROM GOD AND ABSOLUTE SEPARATION FROM THE WORLD (verse 19)

Verse 19 contains two statements, one about John and his readers and the other about the world. Of himself and his readers the apostle asserts, *We know that we are of God* (verse 19a, ASV). That is, the source of our life is in God. Of the world he declares, *the whole world lieth in the evil one* (verse 19b, ASV). That is, it remains in his power, under his influence. Satan is unable to "touch" the Christian, but the world *lies wholly* in his grip. The imagery may be that of a child on a parent's lap.

All men, we may assume, are either "of God" or "in the evil one." There are no other alternatives.

V. THE KNOWLEDGE OF GOD IN CHRIST (verse 20)

The crowning certainty of the Christian is stated in verse 20: *And we know that the Son of God is come, and hath given us an understanding, that we know him that is true, and we are in him that is true, even in his Son Jesus Christ* (ASV). There are three leading thoughts in the verse: (1) that "the Son of God is come," (2) that He is the mediator of our knowledge of God, and (3) that united with Him we are in union with God.

"Is come," which renders a verb found only here in the epistle, stresses Christ's presence *now*. The full meaning is "he has come and is here." Findlay calls attention to its use in John 8:42 ("I came forth from God, *and am come*"). There, he says, it is equivalent to saying "and here I am!" (p. 426).

The result of Christ's coming is that we have "an understanding," that is, a faculty of discerning which makes it possible for us to "know" God. The TCNT says, "We realize, too, that the Son of God has come among us, and has given us the discernment to know the true God."

The Greek word for "know" (second occurrence) is different from the word translated "know" at the beginning of the verse. There it is the word which speaks of absolute knowledge. Here it is the word which denotes knowledge gained by experience. The present tense implies "a continuous and progressive apprehension" (Westcott).

"Him that is true" refers to the Father. The Greek word for "true" signifies that which is genuine as opposed to that which is spurious, that which is real as opposed to that which is counterfeit.

"We are in him that is true" means that we are in vital union with God. The addition of the words "in his Son Jesus Christ" (omit "even" before "in") shows that we are united with the Father by being united with His Son. To know Christ is to know God; to be in Christ is to be in God. "In the experience of the Christian," writes Conner, "fellowship with Christ and fellowship with God are one and inseparable" (p. 196).

This is the true God, and eternal life is not completely clear. Does "this" refer to God the Father or to Jesus Christ? Most modern commentaries seem to prefer the former. The meaning then is that the God revealed and made sure in Christ is the true God and life eternal. We should not, however, reject too readily the view that Jesus Christ is meant, for He is the nearer and more obvious antecedent. Moreover, the connection of thought gives some support to this. In effect, John has just said that to be in the Son is to be in God. How so? Because Christ is Himself very God (Sawtelle). The present writer is unable to choose in a clear-cut way between the two interpretations but leans somewhat to the former. In the final analysis it is not a question of great importance.

To say that God (or Christ) is "eternal life" is to affirm that He is the source of eternal life.

VI. CONCLUSION (verse 21)

Having asserted that in Jesus Christ we have the revelation of "the true God," John concludes with an earnest appeal: *My little children, guard yourselves from idols* (ASV). The verb, appearing only here in the epistle, is used three times in John's gospel (12:25, 47; 17:12). It is found in numerous passages outside of the Johannine writings; for example, in Luke 2:8 of guarding a flock, in I Timothy 6:20 of guarding a deposit, and in Acts 12:4 of guarding a prisoner. The tense (aorist) conveys a note of urgency.

Brooke understands "idols" to embrace "all false conceptions of God" (p. 154). D. Smith thinks the reference is especially to the "heretical [gnostic] substitutes for the Christian conception of God" p. 199). In the broadest sense an idol is whatever "usurps the place of God in the heart, whether this be a person, or a system, or a project, or wealth, or what not" (Plummer, *Pulpit Com.,* p. 144). Conner summarizes as follows: "See to it that you do not try to satisfy your hearts with shams, but let them rest rather in the true, the genuine God who is to be found only in his only begotten Son made flesh for our redemption" (p. 197).

The words of this verse may well have been the last to be written in our Bibles. If so, how solemnly impressive they are!

FOR FURTHER STUDY

1. Underline every occurrence of the word "know" in I John.

2. List the various "tests of life" in I John. See Spurgeon's sermon, "Helps to Full Assurance."

3. Write out in brief statements the teachings of I John on prayer.

4. Divide I John into paragraphs or units and write out in a single sentence what you consider to be the central idea of each paragraph.

Bibliography

Alexander, Neil, *The Epistles of John: Introduction and Commentary* in the "Torch Bible Commentaries" (New York: The Macmillan Company, 1962).

Alexander, W., *The First Epistle General of John* in "The Speaker's Commentary" (New York: Charles Scribner's Sons, 1899).

Alford, Henry, *The New Testament for English Readers* (Chicago: Moody Press, n.d.).

Barclay, William, *The Letters of John and Jude* (Philadelphia: The Westminster Press, 1958).

Barrett, George S., *The First Epistle General of St. John* in "A Devotional Commentary" (London: The Religious Tract Society, n.d.).

Blaiklock, E. M., *Faith Is the Victory: Studies in the First Epistle of John* (Grand Rapids: William B. Eerdmans Publishing Co., 1959).

Brooke, A. E., *A Critical and Exegetical Commentary on the Johannine Epistles* in "The International Critical Commentary" (Edinburgh: T. & T. Clark, 1912).

Calvin, John, *Commentaries on the Catholic Epistles.* Reprint of tr. by John Owen (Grand Rapids: William B. Eerdmans Publishing Co., 1959).

Conner, Walter Thomas, *The Epistles of John: Their Meaning and Message* (New York: Fleming H. Revell Co., 1929).

Dodd, C. H., *The Johannine Epistles* in "The Moffatt New Testament Commentary" (London: Hodder & Stoughton Limited, 1946).

Findlay, George C., *Fellowship in the Life Eternal.* Reprint (Grand Rapids: William B. Eerdmans Publishing Co., 1955).

Hayes, D. A., *John and His Writings* (New York: The Methodist Book Concern, 1917).

Law, Robert, *The Tests of Life: A Study of the First Epistle of St. John* (Edinburgh: T. & T. Clark, 1909).

Orr, R. W., "The Letters of John" in *A New Testament Commentary.* Ed. by G. C. Howley, F. F. Bruce, and H. L. Ellison (Grand Rapids: Zondervan Publishing House, 1969).

Plummer, A., *I John* in "The Pulpit Commentary" (New York: Funk and Wagnalls Co., n.d.).

_____, *The Epistle of St. John* in the "Cambridge Greek Testament for Schools and Colleges" (Cambridge: University Press, 1930).

Ramsay, Alexander, *The Revelation and the Johannine Epistles* in "The Westminster New Testament" (New York: Fleming H. Revell Co., n.d.).

Ross, Alexander, *The Epistles of James and John* in "The New International Commentary on the New Testament" (Grand Rapids: William B. Eerdmans Publishing Co., 1954).

Sawtelle, Henry A., *Commentary on the Epistles of John* in "An American Commentary on the New Testament" (Philadelphia: The American Baptist Publication Society, 1888).

Smith, David, *The Epistles of John* in "The Expositor's Greek Testament" (Grand Rapids: William B. Eerdmans Publishing Company, n.d.).

Spurgeon, Charles H., *The Treasury of the New Testament.* Vol. 4. Reprint (Grand Rapids: Zondervan Publishing House, 1962).

Stott, J. R. W., *The Epistles of John: An Introduction and Commentary* in "The Tyndale New Testament Commentaries" (Grand Rapids: William B. Eerdmans Publishing Co., 1964).

Ward, Ronald A., *The Epistles of John and Jude* (Grand Rapids: Baker Book House, 1965).

Westcott, Brooke Foss, *The Epistles of St. John* (Cambridge: Macmillan and Company, 1892).

The following translations are referred to in this work:

Beck, William F., *The New Testament in the Language of Today* (St. Louis: Concordia Publishing House, 1964).

Goodspeed, Edgar J., *The New Testament; An American Translation* (Chicago: The University of Chicago Press, 1951).

Moffatt, James, *The New Testament; A New Translation* (New York: Harper & Brothers, 1950).

Norlie, Olaf M., *The New Testament: A New Translation* (Grand Rapids: Zondervan Publishing House, 1961).

Phillips, J. B., *The New Testament in Modern English* (New York: The Macmillan Company, 1962).

Weymouth, Richard Francis, *The New Testament in Modern Speech.* Newly revised by James Alexander Robertson (New York: Harper & Brothers, Publishers, n.d.).

Williams, Charles B., *The New Testament: A Private Translation in the Language of the People* (Chicago: Moody Press, 1949).

The Holy Bible: The Berkeley Version in Modern English (Grand Rapids: Zondervan Publishing House, 1959).

The New Englisth Bible: New Testament (Oxford and Cambridge: University Press, 1964). Referred to in the Study Guide as NEB.

Good News for Modern Man: The New Testament in Today's English Version (New York: American Bible Society, n.d.). Referred to in the Study Guide as TEV.

The Holy Bible: Revised Standard Version (New York: American Bible Society, 1952). Referred to in the Study Guide as RSV.

The Holy Bible: Standard Edition (New York: Thomas Nelson & Sons, 1929). Referred to in the Study Guide as ASV.

New American Standard Bible: New Testament (Nashville: Broadman Press, 1963). Referred to in the Study Guide as NASB.

The Twentieth Century New Testament: A Translation into Modern English (Chicago: Moody Press, n.d.). Referred to in the Study Guide as TCNT.